LOST RAILW
NORTH AN
YORKSHIRE

C000292425

Gordon Suggitt

COUNTRYSIDE BOOKS
NEWBURY, BERKSHIRE

First published 2005
© Gordon Suggitt 2005
Reprinted 2006, 2007, 2010

COUNTRYSIDE BOOKS
3 Catherine Road
Newbury, Berkshire

To view our complete range of books,
please visit us at
www.countrysidebooks.co.uk

ISBN 978 1 85306 918 5

Maps and photographs by the author

The cover picture shows Ivatt 4MT Mogul no 43074 at Sandsend
(From an original painting by Colin Doggett)

Produced through MRM Associates Ltd., Reading
Printed by Information Press, Oxford

*All material for the manufacture of this book
was sourced from sustainable forests.*

CONTENTS

Acknowledgements 5

Abbreviations 8

Introduction 9

1 **Around Skipton** 11
Skipton–Bolton Abbey–Ilkley
The Embsay & Bolton Abbey Steam Railway
The Grassington branch

2 **Harrogate Lines** 21
Church Fenton to Harrogate
Harrogate to Ripon, Thirsk and Northallerton
Knaresborough–Boroughbridge – Pilmoor

3 **Nidderdale** 34
The Pateley Bridge branch
The Nidd Valley Light Railway

4 **The Vale of Mowbray** 41
The Easingwold Railway
Melmerby to Masham
The Richmond branch
The Catterick Camp Military Railway

5 **Wensleydale Past and Present** 53
Northallerton–Hawes–Garsdale
The Wensleydale Railway

6 **Cleveland**   60
Picton–Stokesley–Battersby
Middlesbrough to Guisborough
Guisborough to Saltburn and Loftus

7 **Coast Lines**   73
Whitby to Loftus
Scarborough to Whitby
The Filey Holiday Camp branch

8 **Across the North York Moors**   85
Grosmont–Pickering–Malton
The North Yorkshire Moors Railway

9 **The Vale of Pickering**   93
The Forge Valley Line
Pilmoor–Gilling–Malton
Gilling–Pickering

10 **Over the Yorkshire Wolds**   103
Malton to Driffield
York–Market Weighton–Beverley
Selby–Market Weighton–Driffield

11 **Around Selby**   117
Selby to York
The Cawood branch
Selby to Goole
The Derwent Valley Light Railway

12 **Holderness**   131
The Withernsea branch
The Hornsea branch

13 **The Hull & Barnsley Railway**   140
Hull Cannon Street to Carlton Towers

Conclusion   147

Opening and Final Closure Dates   149

Bibliography   151

Index   153

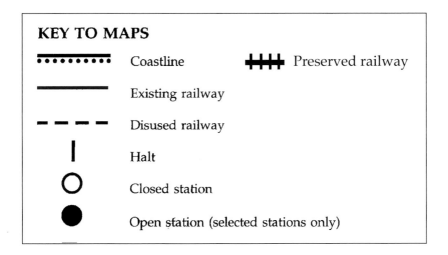

KEY TO MAPS

●●●●●●●●●●● Coastline   ╋╋╋ Preserved railway

━━━━━━━ Existing railway

▬ ▬ ▬ ▬ Disused railway

❙ Halt

○ Closed station

● Open station (selected stations only)

ACKNOWLEDGEMENTS

I would like to acknowledge the help and resources provided by the libraries of North Yorkshire and the East Riding of Yorkshire. I would also like to thank individually John Meredith, Leslie Oppitz and Allan Wood for the use of their photo collections, Syd Walker for the use of his reminiscences and Mike Clark for his help with loco identification. Lastly I am again especially grateful to my wife Jen, who has uncomplainingly visited many of these sites with me, has checked the text with great care and has continued to offer help and encouragement at all times.

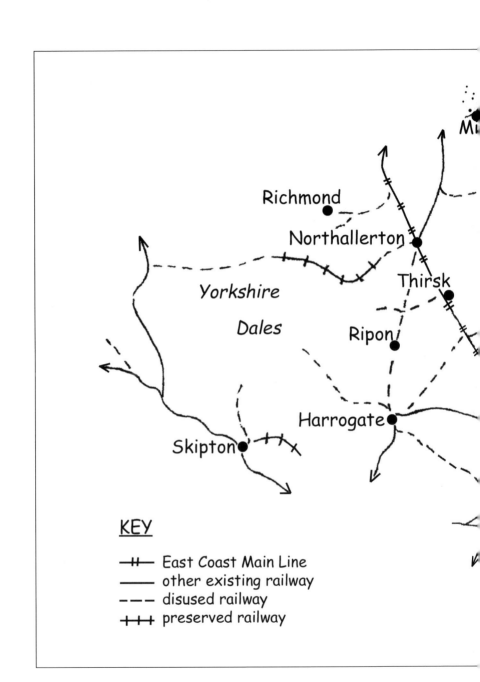

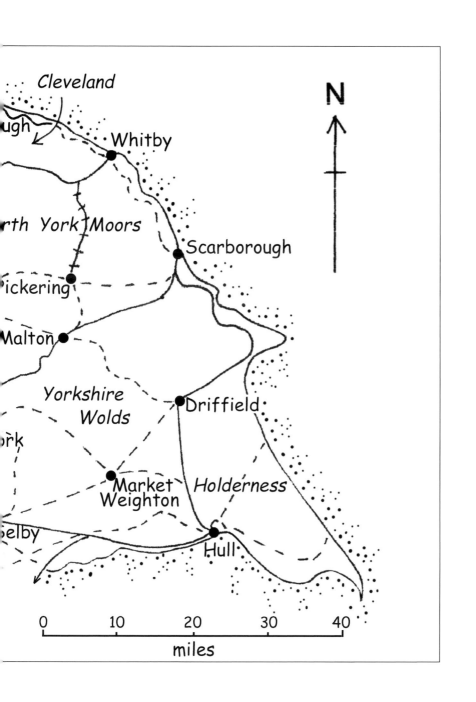

ABBREVIATIONS

The following abbreviations are used in this book:

BR	British Railways
DVLR	Derwent Valley Light Railway
ECML	East Coast Main Line
GNR	Great Northern Railway
H&B	Hull & Barnsley Railway
L&T	Leeds & Thirsk Railway
LMS	London, Midland & Scottish Railway
LN	Leeds Northern Railway
LNER	London & North Eastern Railway
M&D	Malton & Driffield Junction Railway
M&G	Middlesbrough & Guisborough Railway
NER	North Eastern Railway
NVLR	Nidd Valley Light Railway
NY&C	North Yorkshire & Cleveland Railway
RCTS	Railway Correspondence & Travel Society
S&C	Settle & Carlisle
SB&WRJ	Scarborough, Bridlington & West Riding Junction Railway
T&M	Thirsk & Malton
W&P	Whitby & Pickering Railway
WRA	Wensleydale Railway Association
WR&MU	Whitby, Redcar & Middlesbrough Union Railway
Y&NM	York & North Midland Railway

Introduction

'There were giants in the earth in those days' – this Biblical quotation could well be used for the early years of railway history in this area, referring to two 'giants' amongst men, and a railway company. First was George Stephenson, whose Stockton & Darlington Railway of 1825 was extended five years later to Port Darlington, later called Middlesbrough, to provide the area with its first railway. Stephenson was also the engineer for the first line entirely within North and East Yorkshire. This was the Whitby & Pickering Railway, which surprisingly for 1835–6 used horse-drawn carriages throughout except on one incline which was self-operated – steam was not yet in evidence there! This railway incidentally includes all three possibilities for present-day lines – some of it is a 'lost' railway, a stretch is still operational as part of the national network, while a sizeable length has been restored to use as one of the three preservation schemes featured in this book.

In 1836 Stephenson began working with the second 'giant' – George Hudson, the 'Railway King'. Over the next thirteen years up to Hudson's downfall in 1849, the railways reached Yorkshire locations as diverse as Harrogate, York, Scarborough and Hull. Companies controlled by Hudson dominated this expansion, with a total of over 350 miles of track. Within this area, only about 45 miles remained 'independent', chiefly the 30 miles of the Leeds & Thirsk Railway. Even after his fall from power, the companies he had created continued to dominate the area's railways up to 1854. This brings us to the third 'giant', the North Eastern Railway (NER). Formed from three major companies, the Leeds Northern, the York & North Midland, and another former Hudson-controlled company, the York, Newcastle & Berwick (plus, as will be seen later, the tiny Malton & Driffield Railway), this was at the time (1854) the largest railway company in the world. Its influence over this area continued to grow until by the Grouping of 1923 (in which it became a major part of the LNER) it controlled all the railways of North and East Yorkshire, except for three nominally independent minor branch lines and incursions by the Midland into the area's south-western and western extremities.

9

Thus there was some uniformity to the area's rail network found in few other areas of the country, with almost no competing lines and a similarity of style best seen in the stations. Hudson used the York-based architect George Andrews, many of whose distinctive station buildings survive, both in use today as at Scarborough and Hull (Paragon) or reused after their lines' closure, for example at Richmond and Pocklington. However, the NER had a succession of architects and more variation ensued, but there are still some recognisable styles such as Thomas Prosser's stepped gables on the Wensleydale and Pateley Bridge branches, and William Bell's six identical stations on the Forge Valley Line. The NER also left its mark on the pattern of operations in the area, for example, a marked aversion to Sunday services!

It is necessary to more clearly define the lines and area covered by this book. 'Lost railways' have been confined to former standard gauge lines with at one time a regular passenger service, which unfortunately excludes such oddities as the Rosedale mineral line, the Spurn Head Railway and the narrow gauge Sand Hutton Railway (all of these are covered elsewhere – see Bibliography). Other 'out-of-the-ordinary' lines have, however, been included – the light railways in both the Nidd and Derwent valleys, and the branches to the two very different camps at Catterick and Filey. In terms of 'area', some thought was given to using the old North and East Ridings. This would have been historically correct but would have omitted large areas that were in the old West Riding but belong with North and East Yorkshire in terms of their character. So the present-day counties of North Yorkshire and the (new) East Riding of Yorkshire have been used instead, plus the cities of York and Kingston-upon-Hull (henceforth just 'Hull'). This more accurately reflects the division shown in the famous 1949 British Railways map of Yorkshire. There the West Riding is depicted by 'Industry', with 'Farming and Fishing' shown for the North and East Ridings. The map significantly features the coats of arms of just two railway companies, the NER and its successor the LNER. It is thus perhaps ironical that we begin a roughly clockwise coverage of the area's lost railways in the far south-west – with the former Midland and LMS.

Gordon Suggitt

1
Around Skipton

Skipton–Bolton Abbey–Ilkley
The Embsay & Bolton Abbey Steam Railway
The Grassington branch

Midland revival? Present-day Embsay & Bolton Abbey steam operations, although the loco is ex-NCB 'Monckton no 1'. (Author)

Skipton–Bolton Abbey–Ilkley

In the mid 19th century, Skipton was a market town with a population of about 6,000. Its first railway was built by the Leeds & Bradford and opened in 1847. The previous year this company had been leased by the Midland, which absorbed it in 1851. Skipton's railway development continued with lines to Colne in 1848 and to Settle and Ingleton in 1849 (famously extended from

Settle to Carlisle in 1876), and a branch to Ilkley. This did form part of a through route as at Ilkley it met the Midland & NER Joint line to Otley, with further connections to Leeds, Bradford and Harrogate.

The Midland began construction on the 11½ mile Skipton–Ilkley line in 1885, and by the summer of 1888 it was open between Ilkley and Bolton Abbey, one of three intermediate stations. The others were at the villages of Embsay and Addingham (a further one was planned for Draughton but never built). The line was completed through to Skipton by

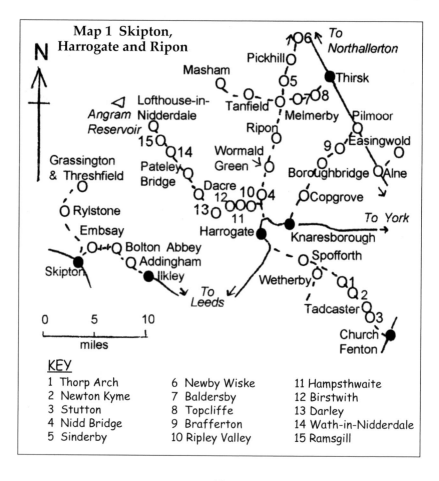

Map 1 Skipton, Harrogate and Ripon

KEY

1 Thorp Arch	6 Newby Wiske	11 Hampsthwaite
2 Newton Kyme	7 Baldersby	12 Birstwith
3 Stutton	8 Topcliffe	13 Darley
4 Nidd Bridge	9 Brafferton	14 Wath-in-Nidderdale
5 Sinderby	10 Ripley Valley	15 Ramsgill

The line was used for through freight workings and passenger diversions, here headed by ex-War Department Austerity class 2-8-0 no 90711. (Travelens Photography)

Monday October 1st 1888, when the first train ran from Colne to Otley. Most services were from Skipton to either Leeds or Bradford, but for a time there were Lancashire & Yorkshire Railway trains from Manchester to Ilkley, replaced by a Midland service from 1908 to 1914. The Midland also ran trains between Skipton and Harrogate in the summers of 1889–1891 and 1913–14, while the NER ran similar summer-only services from York and Harrogate to Bolton Abbey up to 1914. There were also royal arrivals at Bolton Abbey, when the reigning monarch came to stay with the Duke of Devonshire, usually for grouse shooting. Edward VII came in 1902, while George V was a regular visitor and the royal visits ended with George VI in 1947.

Despite its potential to be part of long-distance routes, the line rarely saw regular passenger traffic from outside Yorkshire and Lancashire. On summer Saturdays from 1908 to 1914, there was a Midland train from London St Pancras to Edinburgh, and in the final years of the LNER the line saw a similar summer

13

Saturday service from West Hartlepool to Blackpool and Southport. This continued in BR days, when it was known as the 'Saltburn' from its main portion's starting point, up to the end of the 1963 summer season.

With so little long-distance traffic and its Skipton–Bradford and Leeds services duplicated by those along the Aire valley, it was little surprise that the line did not survive the Beeching Report. Skipton–Ilkley passenger services were withdrawn from 22nd March 1965, and the eastern half through Addingham has largely been lost. However, the section between Embsay and Bolton Abbey has been restored and the 2 miles into Skipton retained for freight workings on the Grassington branch, as will be seen in the next two sections.

The Embsay & Bolton Abbey Steam Railway

Seventy-four years after the name 'Yorkshire Dales Railway' was used for a proposed north–south railway across the Dales, it was revived for a preservation scheme on the former Skipton–Ilkley line. This was in 1969 and the following year the group rented Embsay station and the 800 yards of track leading to it from Embsay Junction, which had been retained to serve a nearby quarry. By 1979 the station, trackbed and track had been purchased, and a steam collection established at the restored Embsay station. The group then concentrated on extending towards Ilkley, reaching a halt and picnic area at Holywell in 1987, when the railway's name was changed to the 'Embsay Steam Railway' (the 'Yorkshire Dales Railway' name has been retained by the trust operating the line). However, the greatest advance was in the 1990s with the purchase of the 2 miles of trackbed leading to the former station at Bolton Abbey, hence the change to the present name. Trains ran to Bolton Abbey in 1997 but it was the next year before the station – a complete rebuild of the distinctive single-storey design erected by the Midland – was opened.

Now trains run throughout the year, though only on Sundays

*Embsay station from the west in the later days of BR ownership.
(Yorkshire Dales Railway Museum collection)*

*A similar view of Embsay today, restored as part of the preserved railway and
in use for a 'Diesel Special Weekend'. (Author)*

The line's more usual stock is well shown by Hunslet 0-6-0ST 'Primrose no 2', with Barclay 0-4-0ST no 22 behind, seen in 1991. (J. Suggitt)

in November, January and most of February and March, and then with increasing frequency through to daily services in late July and August. On summer Saturdays as many as nine return journeys are operated between Embsay and Bolton Abbey. As well as 'Thomas the Tank Engine' weekends, plus Santa trains and 1940s weekends, a special feature is the 'Stately Train' service on summer Sundays, when vintage carriages from the Great North of Scotland Railway and Great Eastern Railway form the stock. Motive power on the line is usually from the railway's stock of mostly ex-industrial steam locos, although on occasions 'Heritage Diesel Multiple Units' are used instead. With 25 years of operation by 2004, this has become one of northern England's most successful railway preservation projects.

The station at Bolton Abbey has been carefully rebuilt in the style created by the Midland for royal visitors (and many less exalted ones). (Author)

The Grassington branch

Wharfedale is the longest of the valleys that together are called the Yorkshire Dales. The 20 or so miles of its upper reaches north of Bolton Abbey attracted seven unsuccessful railway schemes between 1845 and 1895. The last of these, grandly titled the Yorkshire Dales Railway, included a 3½ mile tunnel at the dale's northern end, and would have cost £1.5 million to reach Darlington from the Settle & Carlisle line at Hellifield. This failed like all its predecessors, but two years later in 1897 its promoters tried again with a more modest scheme to tap the minerals of the Grassington area. This resulted in an 8½ mile single-track branch from Embsay Junction, east of Skipton, built for £72,000.

The line had one intermediate station at Rylstone. Its terminus was ½ mile short of Grassington village, so avoiding the expense of crossing the River Wharfe, and was on the edge of the

17

Grassington station building, seen here around 1910, was constructed by the Portable Buildings Company for a cost of £279. (Stations UK)

separate village of Threshfield, hence its eventual title of 'Grassington & Threshfield'. Construction began in 1900 and was done on the cheap, without the planned passing loop at Rylstone or turntable at the terminus, which was, however, built as a through station with two platforms in the vain hope of further expansion up the valley. The branch was operated from the start by the Midland, including the train for the opening ceremony on 29th July 1902, when Johnson 0-4-4T no 1536 hauled between 200 and 300 guests to the terminus, where it was met by a procession from the village including the local constabulary, Parish Council, Temperance Band and decorated carts. Services reached a peak of six or seven weekday trains in 1913, one including a carriage from Bradford, with two trains on Sundays. In 1922, when the line was finally absorbed by the Midland, the service was similar but passengers were already being lost to buses serving Grassington village centre. In 1930 the branch became one of 23 to be closed by the LMS, with passenger services withdrawn from 22nd September. Excursions, important since the line's opening, did continue to run, often causing huge problems at the inadequate terminus. At

For many years after closure to scheduled passenger services, the Grassington terminus was visited by excursions such as this one from Manchester Victoria in 1952. (C.H.A. Townley, courtesy J.A. Peden)

Excursions continue though only as far as the Swinden limestone quarry. This was the 'Cracoe Jack' railtour from London King's Cross in November 2003. (Author)

Easter 1949, for example, there were three excursion trains (from Leeds, Bradford and Huddersfield) there at the same time, all needing to be sorted for the return journey including the three locos' trips back to Skipton for coal and water! Such visits continued well into the 1960s, but the last 1½ miles of track at the Grassington end closed in 1969 and the station site was cleared. However, occasional excursions do still traverse the rest of the branch.

Mineral traffic was one of the reasons for the line's construction. By 1905 huge quarries at Swinden and Skythorn were sending out vast quantities of lime, necessitating the passing loop as originally planned at Rylstone. This traffic and local freight continued to be steam-hauled until summer 1968, attracting many enthusiasts to what was described as 'Britain's last steam-worked branch line'. Freight to the terminus ended the following year, but the line continues to see diesel workings to Swinden Quarry.

2
Harrogate Lines

Church Fenton to Harrogate
Harrogate to Ripon, Thirsk and Northallerton
Knaresborough–Boroughbridge–Pilmoor

For many years up to 1964 the 'Queen of Scots' Pullman was the prestige train through Harrogate. Here it is hauled by Gresley-designed A3 4-6-2 no 60084 'Trigo'. (Author's collection)

Church Fenton to Harrogate

In 1848 the Editor of the *Harrogate Advertiser* wished for the invention of steam wings so that visitors could get to the famous spa town more easily! Not surprisingly he had to settle instead for steam trains, which did reach the town that year. These were

21

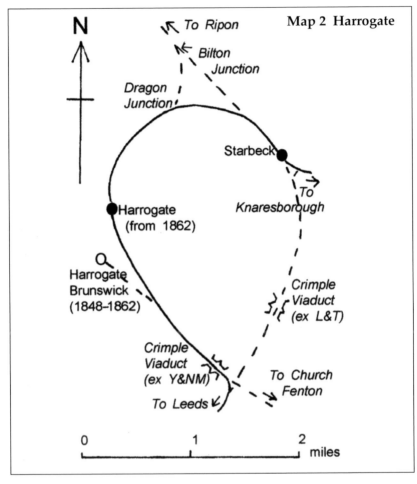

N

↑

To Ripon

Bilton Junction

Dragon Junction

Map 2 Harrogate

Starbeck

To Knaresborough

Harrogate (from 1862)

Harrogate Brunswick (1848-1862)

Crimple Viaduct (ex L&T)

Crimple Viaduct (ex Y&NM)

To Leeds

To Church Fenton

0   1   2 miles

on George Hudson's York & North Midland Railway (Y&NM) branch from Church Fenton to Harrogate's first station, called Brunswick after a nearby hotel. It was built at a corner of the Stray, the town's grassy open space, and included buildings from a farm previously on the site. The line had opened to Spofforth in the previous year, 1847, and passengers were conveyed the 5 miles to Harrogate by horse-drawn omnibus. The final stretch into the town was opened suddenly and without ceremony on 20th July 1848, and a service of five weekday trains each way began (there were never any scheduled Sunday services).

Within two years this was down to three a day, probably due to the arrival of a second railway, the Leeds & Thirsk, promoted by a group of Leeds businessmen. It opened only eight weeks after the Y&NM, but its station for Harrogate was at Starbeck, 1¾ miles to the east. When completed to Leeds in July 1849, this line provided a much more direct service without the need for connections at Church Fenton. The formation of the NER in 1854 led to major improvements for Harrogate, notably a new station centrally placed for the town. This opened in August 1862, and as its line also crossed the Stray, the NER agreed to return the Brunswick station site to open space. Thus by 1864 Harrogate's first station had disappeared.

Trains to Church Fenton were back to five each way by 1880, most calling at the intermediate stations of Spofforth, Wetherby, Thorp Arch (for Boston Spa), Newton Kyme, Tadcaster and Stutton. By then Wetherby was linked to Cross Gates, east of Leeds. However, the line was single-track and the connection only towards Church Fenton. In 1901 this link was doubled, with a curve towards Harrogate and a new Wetherby station (replacing the previous one on the Harrogate–Church Fenton line, which became the goods station). This led to a concentration of traffic on the Harrogate–Wetherby section of the ex-Y&NM line, most trains continuing to Leeds.

Some trains covered the eastern section from Wetherby to Church Fenton, but little traffic now ran through from Harrogate to Church Fenton, the exception being the London expresses. These began in 1902 with three daily GNR trains to and from King's Cross, and such services continued after the Grouping in 1923 including for a time the prestigious 'Harrogate Pullman'. Some people say that this was the route used by Agatha Christie for her disappearance to Harrogate in 1926. However, the line was always second-best for such expresses compared with the former Leeds & Thirsk route through Bramhope Tunnel, and all Harrogate–London services via Church Fenton ended by 1947.

Stutton station, only ½ mile from Tadcaster, closed to passengers in 1905, but a new station opened for Wetherby Racecourse in 1924. At Thorp Arch in 1942 a 6½ mile single-track

Newton Kyme station in 1962, with the RCTS 'East Midlander' railtour here headed by an unusual sight on Yorkshire rails – ex-Southern Railway Schools class no 30925 'Cheltenham'. (Author's collection)

Another rare sighting as streamlined A4 4-6-2 no 60034 'Lord Faringdon' brings a diverted train off the Tadcaster branch at Chaloner Whin, south of York. (Author's collection)

The station building at Newton Kyme was designed by George Andrews for the York & North Midland Railway and has been splendidly preserved. (Author, courtesy R. Wade)

circuit with four stations was opened for a munitions factory, served by workers' trains from as far away as Hull and Doncaster, which continued in use until 1958. By then there were only two local trains between Harrogate and Wetherby and one Church Fenton–Wetherby train. The Wetherby–Harrogate section remained busy with Leeds–Newcastle passenger traffic and freight to and from Teesside, but the latter would soon end with the quadrupling of the East Coast Main Line north of York. Wetherby Racecourse station closed in 1959, though race excursions continued to use the town's station. However, the passenger services – what little was left of them – were the first to be withdrawn after Beeching, Harrogate–Church Fenton and Wetherby–Cross Gates closing on 6th January 1964, although goods traffic continued on the Wetherby–Church Fenton section until 1966.

Sections of the route are now used as cycle trails, principally the 3 miles of former trackbed between Spofforth and Wetherby,

One railway survival at Tadcaster is this eleven-arch viaduct over the River Wharfe, constructed in the 1840s for a York & North Midland line that was never built. (Author)

while station buildings survive at Newton Kyme, Thorp Arch and Stutton, although Tadcaster station has been lost to redevelopment. At Harrogate a mile of the original 1848 route takes the present-day line from Leeds across the Crimple valley, still using the massive 31-arch viaduct built by the Y&NM. Ironically this crosses a section of the former Leeds & Thirsk route to Starbeck, abandoned since 1951.

Harrogate to Ripon, Thirsk and Northallerton

Harrogate's second railway, the Leeds and Thirsk (L&T) was built south from Thirsk, reaching the small cathedral city of Ripon by January 1848. The station was almost a mile from the centre (they were linked in 1904 by one of the country's first motorbus services) and was regarded as a temporary location but was never replaced. Passenger services began on 31st May 1848 when special trains ran, including one of 20 carriages carrying over 500 passengers, plus the navvies' band and a Ripon brass band. Public services began the next day with four daily trains each way, two on Sundays. As well as Ripon and Thirsk, stations were provided at Wath, Baldersby and Topcliffe. The line was extended south from Ripon in stages, through stations at Wormald Green and Nidd Bridge (Ripley up to 1862) to Starbeck (for Harrogate), finally reaching Leeds in July 1849.

The final destination of the L&T was Stockton-on-Tees, but the company was persuaded by George Hudson to use the line of his Great North of England Railway (present-day East Coast Main Line) from Thirsk to Northallerton. In 1851 the L&T changed its name to the Leeds Northern (LN) and the following year opened its own line from Wath, now called Melmerby, north through stations at Sinderby, Pickhill and Newby Wiske to Northallerton. There the LN ran under the main line to its separate station and on to Stockton. However, in 1856 a curve was added allowing trains from Stockton to join the main line to Thirsk. The LN stations at Thirsk and Northallerton closed to passengers (but stayed open for goods) and the Melmerby–

York-based class A1 4-6-2 no 60146 'Peregrine', seen here north of Harrogate, worked the 'Queen of Scots' Pullman in 1953 which made a special stop at Ripon for the Queen Mother. (Author's collection)

Northallerton line became a single-track branch.

The route benefited from the NER's impovements at Harrogate in 1862, with a curve from Bilton Junction to Dragon Junction leading to the new central station, while in 1901 the line north from Melmerby was doubled and connected to the main line northbound at Northallerton. The Melmerby–Northallerton line now took more through traffic at the expense of the route via Thirsk. By 1922 fourteen northbound trains a day called at Ripon, including two Liverpool–Newcastle services and a GNR express from King's Cross. Intermediate stations fared less well, with only two or three trains a day at Sinderby, Newby Wiske (which closed to passengers in 1939), Baldersby and Topcliffe, and four trains a week at Pickhill.

After World War II local services continued to decline and ended altogether on the Melmerby–Thirsk section in 1959, although freight at the former L&T Thirsk terminus continued for another seven years. Pickhill station also shut in 1959, followed by Sinderby in 1961, and Nidd Bridge and Wormald

The station at Ripon has been well restored as residences, including the stationmaster's house in the foreground. (Author)

The much more humble Wormald Green station, seen here with its staff in NER days, has also been restored. (Lens of Sutton Association)

Green the next year. Only Ripon and Melmerby stations were still open for passengers when the line through to Northallerton was listed for closure in the Beeching Report. The widening of the East Coast Main Line by 1959 had meant there was no longer any need for an alternative through route, especially for freight, and despite vigorous opposition from the residents of Ripon, passenger services were withdrawn on 6th March 1967. Freight continued to Ripon until 1969, and the line was lifted the following year. At the southern end, short stretches of the lines into Harrogate and Starbeck are in use as cycle routes, but north of Ripon little remains; much of the trackbed has disappeared and the once-important junction station at Melmerby has left not a trace.

Knaresborough–Boroughbridge–Pilmoor

This has been included with 'Harrogate Lines' as it was usually worked from Harrogate, although only the section from Knaresborough counts as a 'lost railway'. In the 1840s there were proposals for a line through the small town of Boroughbridge, a coaching stop on the old Great North Road. This was to run from Pilmoor on the York–Darlington line (the present East Coast Main Line) to Knaresborough and Harrogate. Eventually in 1847 the Great North of England Railway opened a branch from Pilmoor to Boroughbridge, with an intermediate station at Brafferton.

The connection to Knaresborough was proposed again in 1865 but it was another ten years before it was finally built by the NER. It had taken over thirty years for the original proposal to be completed! Even then its usefulness was limited as a southbound connection at Pilmoor was never built, nor was a connection to the Thirsk & Malton Railway ever used. The Boroughbridge line was left as a quiet, rural branch with only northbound access onto the main line at a branch platform at Pilmoor, a remote railway community with at one time seventeen dwellings, plus a shop, church and reading room. The Knaresborough extension required a new station at

Brafferton station in 1960 with a Harrogate–Pilmoor train headed by class G5 0-4-4T no 67289, which as NER class O no 1911 had been the Masham branch loco up to 1930. (Author's collection)

Boroughbridge, built at a higher level to allow for a crossing of the River Ure (the old station remained in use for goods until 1964). A new intermediate station was also built at Copgrove and Staveley (although the 'and Staveley' was later dropped to avoid confusion with Staveley in Derbyshire).

Typical services were those in 1936 when there was a single passenger train operating Harrogate–Pilmoor and return services twice daily Mondays to Fridays, with two extra return journeys on Saturdays. There was also one daily 'pick-up' goods train each way, and a weekly cattle train. With the route through Ripon just to the west, there were few diversions on this line, but occasional excursions and regular test runs of newly built locos from Darlington (out via Ripon, back by Boroughbridge). The line was at its busiest during World War II, with materials and parts for Dishforth airfield, and particularly ammunition to and from the 'shell dump' near Brafferton. It is estimated that this

Pilmoor station with the East Coast Main Line at the left, while on the right G5 no 67337 waits with a train from Harrogate (this loco hauled the last-ever such train in 1950). (Author's collection)

While the later station at Boroughbridge has vanished, the stationmaster's house of the earlier (1847) station is used by brick retailers. (Author)

amounted to 250,000 tons of bombs moved between 1941 and 1947.

After the war the line was soon a candidate for closure, with journeys from its stations averaging only three per train. BR applied to close it to passengers in April 1950, claiming this would save £6,387 a year. Many enthusiasts travelled the line in its final week, especially the last day of all, 23rd September 1950. Goods services between Pilmoor and Brafferton ended at the same time, but lasted another 14 years from Knaresborough to Brafferton. Although Brafferton and the later Boroughbridge station have disappeared completely, Copgrove station and four crossing keepers' cottages remain as residences. However, the most surprising survival is the stationmaster's house at the original Boroughbridge station, dating back to 1847.

3
Nidderdale

The Pateley Bridge branch
The Nidd Valley Light Railway

The last steam working in Nidderdale was an enthusiasts' special in
October 1963 hauled by Fowler class 4P 2-6-4T no 42409, seen here at
Pateley Bridge. (Author's collection)

The Pateley Bridge branch

Nidderdale is the quietest of the Yorkshire Dales and an unlikely
possible location for the world's first steam railway. In 1820, five
years before the opening of the Stockton & Darlington Railway,
Thomas Telford proposed a railway rather than a canal to
Knaresborough, with an extension to Pateley Bridge. Nothing

Pateley Bridge station building, with its distinctive stepped gable, around 1900. (Lens of Sutton, courtesy L. Oppitz)

The same style of architecture could be seen down-valley at Dacre station. (Stations UK)

came of this proposal, nor one from the Leeds & Thirsk Railway in 1848, and it was left to the NER to obtain an Act for the branch in 1859. Construction began in September 1860 and the line opened on 1st May 1862. It left the former Leeds & Thirsk route at Ripley Junction north of Harrogate, and followed the valley for 11½ miles up to its major settlement, the small town of Pateley Bridge.

The branch was single-track, with passing places at the intermediate stations of Killinghall (Ripley Valley from 1875), Birstwith and Dacre. Services were initially four return journeys to Harrogate on weekdays, including stops at additional stations provided at Darley in 1864 and Hampsthwaite two years later. In 1892, the line was severely affected by flooding, when Ripley Valley station became an island, outgoing mail was taken to Pateley Bridge station by raft and the first train to get through took over three hours for the forty minute journey to Harrogate.

By 1923 weekday return journeys had increased to seven, most worked by a single engine kept at Pateley Bridge, ex-NER class G5 0-4-4T no 1839. Ten years later, services were down to

The well-restored Dacre station building in 2004. (Author)

36

four a day, but there were three extra trains on Saturdays and two on Sundays, with summer Sunday through trains from Leeds in 1939. Hampsthwaite station closed in 1950, when there were only two weekday return journeys and one more on Saturdays. BR applied to close the line that year and despite local protests, the last train ran on 31st March 1951. This was hauled by the same class G5 loco as used in the 1920s, now renumbered 67253. Occasional excursions and goods traffic continued for another thirteen years, the latter finishing on 30th October 1964. Since then several stations have been demolished, notably Birstwith and Darley, but the station buildings at Pateley Bridge and Dacre survive.

The Nidd Valley Light Railway

From 1907 there was a second station in Pateley Bridge, serving a separate line leading further up Nidderdale. Although the two lines were connected for freight, passengers had to walk over ¼ mile through the streets from the NER station to the terminus of the Nidd Valley Light Railway (NVLR). This line was first proposed as a 2 ft 6 inch gauge railway in 1901, the same year that Gouthwaite, the first of three Nidderdale reservoirs for Bradford, was completed. Nothing came of this proposal and it was left to Bradford Corporation to take over the powers for the line in 1904. The plans were changed to standard gauge, together with the conversion of the 3 ft gauge line already built by the contractors up the valley from the village of Lofthouse to the site of the second reservoir at Angram. The original Light Railway order had included provision for passenger services between Pateley Bridge and Lofthouse, and so Bradford Corporation became the first municipal owner of a public railway in Britain.

On Wednesday, 14th July 1904, a party of 150 councillors, officials and guests travelled by train from Bradford for the inauguration of both the NVLR and Angram Reservoir. Three years later, 11th September 1907 saw the line's opening ceremony. The train from Pateley Bridge to Lofthouse consisted of three carriages and Bradford Corporation's private saloon, all

The line's engine no 1, 0-4-4T 'Holdsworth', leaving Lofthouse-in-Nidderdale station for Pateley Bridge with six ex-Metropolitan Railway four-wheeled coaches. (Lens of Sutton, courtesy L. Oppitz)

hauled by a loco driven by Bradford's Lord Mayor – probably another municipal 'first'! Next day public services began with four return journeys daily, taking twenty minutes for the 6½ mile journey. Return fares were 2/- first class and 1/- third class although excursion fares of 9d soon proved popular. Two-storey, stone-built stations were provided at Pateley Bridge, Wath, Ramsgill and Lofthouse (which along with Wath added '-in-Nidderdale' to avoid confusion with other locations in Yorkshire). Two 4-4-0 Beyer Peacock locos and ten four-wheeled carriages had been purchased from the Metropolitan Railway, although goods stock was bought new.

By 1910 the line was carrying over 45,000 passengers and 13,000 tons of goods a year. Angram Reservoir was completed in 1915 but services continued through World War I, reducing to three trains each way in 1918. They were increased to five by 1922, but by then the stations had closed, though trains still called 'by request'. This contributed to a 30% decline in passenger numbers between 1921 and 1925, although the completion of work on a 'village' for the third reservoir at Scar House greatly reduced workmen's journeys. (The village housed over 1,000 people in ten hostels and 62 bungalows, and included

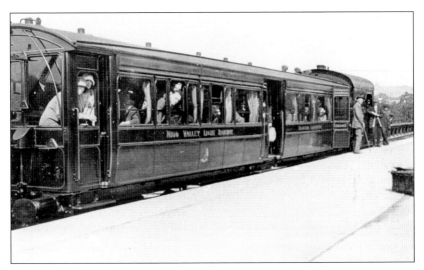

Kerr Stuart steam railmotor 'Hill', built in 1905 for the GWR, saw service on the NVLR in the 1920s. (J.A. Peden collection)

The NVLR's Pateley Bridge station (with its building in the centre background) in 1957, over twenty years after the line's closure. (C.H.A. Townley, courtesy J.A. Peden)

a canteen, a recreation hall, a block of six shops, a hospital and a school.) Excursions to the upper dale were now increasingly by 'charabanc' and in June 1929 Bradford's Waterworks Committee decided to end scheduled passenger services over the line. This was on 31st December 1929 without ceremony – the closure wasn't even reported in any of the Bradford newspapers.

Many excursions continued to use the line to see the continuing work on Scar House Reservoir, but once this was completed in 1936 the line was soon closed and all equipment, including the remaining locos, auctioned off. Despite the line's construction as a light railway, much of its route can still be seen and stretches are still walkable north of Pateley Bridge and alongside Gouthwaite Reservoir, while the former station buildings at Wath, Ramsgill and Lofthouse remain as private residences.

4
The Vale of Mowbray

The Easingwold Railway
Melmerby to Masham
The Richmond branch
The Catterick Camp Military Railway

The pick-up goods train of yesteryear is captured in this scene near Melmerby with class A6 4-6-2T no 69794; this class had been well represented at Whitby, hence the nickname 'Whitby Willies'! (Author's collection)

The Easingwold Railway

The name 'Vale of Mowbray' refers to the plain between York and Darlington, with the Yorkshire Dales to the west and the

North York Moors to the east. It provides the setting for four short lines, two of them NER branches and two independent lines. One of the latter was the Easingwold Railway, sometimes called England's shortest standard gauge passenger railway, which at only 2½ miles may well be true for an independent line rather than a branch. It was built to connect the village of Easingwold to the East Coast Main Line at Alne, 11 miles north of York, and was independently owned by the Easingwold Railway Company. The cost of the railway was almost £17,000, including rolling stock, as against the original estimate of £10,000. The Board of Trade inspector described it as 'more or less a tram road' and restricted speeds to 12 mph while the company's only locomotive (soon replaced) was a tiny 0-4-0 tank engine.

The opening day was Saturday 25th July 1891, when local children were given free rides to and from Alne. Initially passenger services were nine return journeys per day, though not on Sundays, and there were still seven per day as late as 1939. However, goods traffic, chiefly agricultural, was the

The Easingwold Railway Company's loco no 2 was its sole engine between 1903 and 1947. (Travelens Photography)

mainstay of the line and allowed the company to stay in profit until the late 1920s, when the staff consisted of two drivers (who also doubled as guards), one fireman, a stationmaster, two clerks, four porters, two platelayers and the shed cat! The company only ever owned and ran one loco at a time, Hudswell Clarke saddle tanks doing the job up to 1947, when a loco was hired from the LNER and later BR.

The railway kept its independence through both the Grouping of 1923 and nationalisation, though passenger services were down to two per day by 1946. In 1947 the number of passengers averaged only twelve a week and ticket sales for the whole year totalled £18, so the service was withdrawn on 29th November 1948. Goods traffic lingered on but between 1949 and 1956 expenses trebled, with the cost of hiring a loco alone rising to £40 a week. Income over the same period went down by 28% and the line was losing £1,700 a year. The end came on Friday 27th December 1957, after which the company went into voluntary liquidation with debts of £17,000. Within two years Alne station

After 1947, the company hired locos from BR such as this class J71 0-6-0T, no 68313, waiting at Alne's bay platform with a single coach for Easingwold. (Real Photographs)

The last railtour to visit Easingwold was the RCTS 'Yorkshire Coast Rail Tour' on 23rd June 1957, seen here with J71 no 68246. (Author's collection)

had been closed and demolished for main line modernisation, while Easingwold's station building lasted until 1967 when it was destroyed by fire, leaving only the Station Hotel as a reminder of 66 years of railway history.

Melmerby to Masham

In the late 19th century Masham was a small town with less than 1,000 people and a market place, but no market until the railway arrived! Its 7¾ mile single-track branch line was all that was built of a proposal for an east–west railway across the Yorkshire Dales. Worried that other companies might gain access to its territory, in 1865 the NER backed the Hawes & Melmerby Railway, only to later decide to build from Hawes to Leyburn instead. To recompense the inhabitants of the area between Melmerby and Leyburn, the NER agreed to build the Masham branch, which opened on 9th June 1875. A passing loop was

Tanfield station in the early years of the 20th century, with a good turnout on the platform! (Lens of Sutton Association)

Despite being described as derelict in 1973, Tanfield station has now been well restored. (Author)

provided at the sole intermediate station of Tanfield, while the terminus had a single road engine shed, which housed the branch's solitary engine, class O no 1911, in the years up to 1930. A weekday service of four trains a day was operated to Ripon and back before closure to passengers on 30th December 1930, when it was replaced by a bus service operated by the LNER. The line had been busiest between 1901 and the mid-1920s, while Harrogate and Leeds Corporations built reservoirs south-west of Masham. From 1905 a 2 ft gauge railway led from Masham station to the reservoir depot. After closure to passengers the Masham branch kept freight traffic for another 33 years, usually worked by a daily pick-up goods train from Starbeck. The line was particularly busy during World War II, with 42 trains to an ammunition storage depot at Tanfield in the six weeks up to D-Day alone. Traffic fell away after 1945 and it is surprising that final closure did not come until 11th November 1963. Little is left of the line but both station buildings survive.

The Richmond branch

Although regarded as a NER branch, the 10 mile branch to this historic market town was built by the Great North of England Railway and opened in 1846. The aim was to tap the lead-mining areas of Swaledale and although schemes were put forward for extensions beyond Richmond as late as 1912 nothing came of them and the line remained a rural branch. It left the East Coast Main Line at Eryholme Junction (Dalton Junction up to 1901) where there was a station until 1911, and there were further stations at Moulton, Scorton and Catterick Bridge before a 'handsome little station' across from Richmond on the south bank of the River Swale. The railway company had to build a four-arch bridge over the river for access to the town.

The line opened on 10th September 1846 with three trains each way. Most early services were between Richmond and Eryholme until the closure of the latter station. Croft Spa on the main line was then used as the interchange for a time, but by 1922 services from Richmond ran through to Darlington. These

46

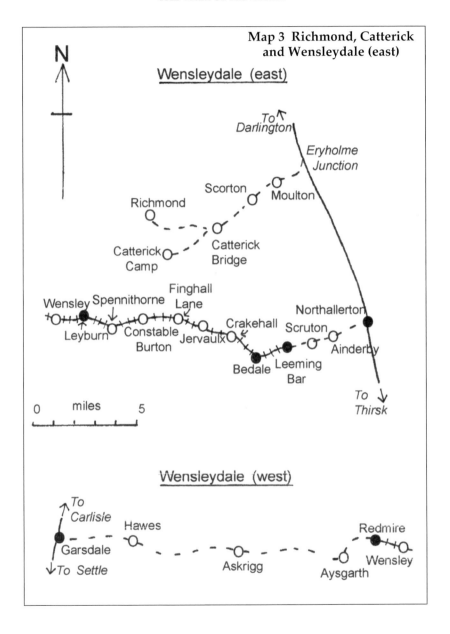

Map 3 Richmond, Catterick and Wensleydale (east)

A splendid interior view of Richmond station, with a pair of the diesel units that handled the service from Darlington after 1958. (J.H. Meredith)

Richmond station's exterior was looking distinctly shabby by February 1969, only a month before closure. (J.H. Meredith)

consisted of six return journeys on weekdays, with an extra Saturday train, and two trains each way on Sundays. There was also excursion traffic, especially for Richmond's Whit Monday 'Athletic Sports and Bicycle Meet'. As early as 1892 this event saw specials from Middlesbrough, Saltburn and Bishop Auckland, plus relief trains from Darlington. Despite the proximity of the Catterick Camp branch, many troop trains ran to Richmond instead, especially during World War II, when Gresley-designed A3 and V2 locos were commonly seen. There was a major accident on the line in 1944 when ammunition being loaded into railway wagons at Catterick Bridge station exploded, killing twelve people including the stationmaster.

By 1960 there were twelve daily trains, with an extra one on Mondays and Saturdays and three on Sundays, but BR claimed the branch ran at a loss and in 1963 applied for closure apart from certain military trains. This was refused, but after the line was singled BR tried again in 1968, and this time, despite local objections, approval was given so the line closed on 3rd March 1969. Freight traffic to Catterick Bridge continued for another

The former Richmond station, designed by George Andrews and opened in 1846, was a disused building when photographed in June 2004. (Author)

eleven months but later in 1970 the line was dismantled. Its chief remnant is the listed Richmond station building, in use as a garden centre for many years until 2003, but there are plans for its reuse as a community centre.

The Catterick Camp Military Railway

Around 1908 Lord Baden Powell, founder of the Boy Scout movement, suggested the Richmond area for a modern military camp, but it was 1914 before anything was done. Within weeks of the outbreak of World War I, surveyors told local residents on the Scotton Hall Estate that they were surveying the line of a railway for a 'new camp'. Soon afterwards a 2 ft gauge construction line was laid from the Richmond branch west of Catterick Bridge, climbing 300 ft in its first 3 miles towards the

The basic facilities at Catterick's Camp Centre station in the 1950s, with ex-GCR class A5 4-6-2T no 69806. (L.A. Strudwick)

50

camp site. The line was completed by May 1915 and converted to standard gauge by the end of the year. The camp was first called Richmond Camp, but the name was changed to avoid confusion with Richmond, Surrey. It was originally designed for two divisions, totalling 40,000 men, and admitted its first soldiers in October 1916, with 750,000 passing through each year until the end of the war. The military authorities then decided to make the camp permanent, and in 1923 handed over the running of its railway to the LNER, with BR responsible from 1948.

The line's course began at a junction that only faced towards Richmond. Almost immediately a platform was built at Brampton Road, which allowed access to Catterick Bridge station, followed by a three-span girder bridge over the River Swale. After the bridge the line climbed to the camp's main station, called Camp Centre. Before 1923 the line had continued to a further station named California, just over 5 miles from Catterick Bridge, but it was cut back by the LNER to the camp's Power House. This was ½ mile beyond Camp Centre and involved trains passing through

The three-span girder bridge over the River Swale is the line's chief remaining feature. (Author)

the middle of a road roundabout.

Initially there were freight trains and troop specials from the East Coast Main Line, with local and leave traffic handled by passenger services from the camp to Brampton Road platform, for Catterick Bridge. During World War II the latter were revived, with some trains through to Darlington, services reaching a peak of 3–4 on weekdays and 5 on Sundays in late 1945. After this passenger services became restricted to weekend leave trains and by the late 1950s these were down to a Friday afternoon departure for Newcastle and one at Saturday lunchtime for London, with three early Monday morning trains back from Darlington. A serviceman's return to London in 1955 cost 36/8d, compared with over £4 for a 'civilian', although the latter was likely to receive more than the soldier's 20/- a week! Passenger services to the camp ended on 26th October 1964, although access was still possible from Richmond or Catterick Bridge for another five years. By October 1970 the branch had been dismantled and has left little trace of its existence except for the bridge over the River Swale.

5
Wensleydale Past and Present

Northallerton–Hawes–Garsdale
The Wensleydale Railway

Class G5 no 67345 (which hauled the last-ever scheduled passenger train over the line from Northallerton to Leyburn and back, on Sunday 25th April 1954) is seen here at Scruton. (Author's collection)

Northallerton–Hawes–Garsdale

Wensleydale is the broadest east–west valley in the Yorkshire Dales, and attracted numerous 19th century railway builders with schemes to link the east and west coast main lines. In the 'Railway Mania' of the 1840s four such projects got as far as

Parliamentary bills. The 1860s saw three more schemes and by 1878 Wensleydale did have its own railway, but it had been built in stages, was owned by two separate companies and was only a rural branch line! Construction had begun as early as 1847 with the Newcastle & Darlington Junction Railway's Bedale branch, and even this 7½ mile line heading west from the present-day East Coast Main Line at Northallerton was not completed without problems. The collapse of George Hudson's empire meant that only the 6 miles to Leeming were completed by 1848. That remained the terminus until the Bedale & Leyburn Railway, backed by the newly formed NER, extended the line to Bedale in 1855, and to Leyburn the following year with a passenger service of four or five trains a day.

The Midland Railway's Settle & Carlisle (S&C) Bill of 1866 included, for the upper part of the dale, a branch from Garsdale to Hawes, where it would link with one of the many schemes for the valley, the Hawes & Melmerby Railway. This was dropped in favour of a Hawes–Leyburn link to the branch from Northallerton, owned by the NER since 1859. Despite the Midland's attempts to

Ainderby station, like all the stations as far as Bedale, was a George Andrews design. It survives but the signal box was removed for use on the South Tynedale Railway at Alston. (Author's collection)

54

Constable Burton station shows a more typical NER stepped-gable design, seen here with class G5 no 67314. (Author's collection)

abandon the S&C scheme, construction of both its link to Hawes and the NER connection went ahead and Wensleydale at last had its 'through' railway, opened to passenger traffic on 1st October 1878. The completed line totalled nearly 40 miles, almost 6 miles of which were owned by the Midland Railway. These ran from Garsdale station (Hawes Junction before 1933) on the S&C main line to Hawes, where the station was built to a Midland design. The NER owned the remainder of the branch, with stations at Ainderby, Scruton, Leeming Lane (Leeming Bar from 1902), Bedale, Crakehall, Jervaulx (Newton-le-Willows until 1877), Finghall Lane, Constable Burton, Spennithorne, Leyburn, Wensley, Redmire, Aysgarth and Askrigg. Passenger services were four or five trains in each direction, operated by the NER to the western 'terminus' at Garsdale, and additionally in the 1900s a daily Midland train (known by railwaymen as the 'Bonnyface') from Hellifield to Hawes.

The line served sparsely populated rural areas and was never well used. Its peak service was in the early 20th century with seven trains each way on weekdays, although Sundays saw only a single down-valley train from Hawes. Usage continued to grow until the early 1920s, but then declined with increased motor transport and continued population loss from the dale. Both companies operated daily goods trains; the NER freight roster included limestone trains and milk shipments, over ½ million gallons in 1906. After 1923, the line was still operated by two companies, the LMS west of Hawes and the LNER to the east, and passenger services continued at four or five trains a day, with the solitary Sunday train no longer advertised by 1939. A major 'event' on the line had been the full eclipse of the sun on 29th June 1927, for which the LNER decided that Leyburn (along with Richmond) would be an ideal viewing location. Hundreds of people arrived on special trains from as far afield as Nottingham, Colchester and London; unfortunately the weather rather spoilt the viewing, being partially overcast.

World War II saw increased usage, especially to RAF Leeming, and nationalisation in 1948 meant the whole line became part of BR's North Eastern Region, though ex-LMS stock continued to work the 'Bonnyface' service from Garsdale to Hawes. However BR applied to end the Hawes–Northallerton passenger service in 1953, claiming that only 2½% of the dale's residents used the trains and that closure would save £14,500 a year. Despite protests, closure for passengers was announced for Monday 26th April 1954. A single weekday Garsdale–Hawes return passenger working lasted for another five years and freight was only gradually run down, finishing finally on 31st May 1982 – with one exception. The movement of limestone from Redmire to Teesside steel mills continued, involving shipments of 2,000 tons six days a week by 1989. Occasional passenger specials visited the line, latterly only as far as Redmire. However, in December 1992 British Steel ended the movement of Redmire stone by train, and the remaining 22 miles of track to Northallerton went out of regular use.

'No Sympathy Wanted' is scrawled on class D20 4-4-0 no 62347 at Hawes on the last day of services from Northallerton, Saturday 24th April 1954. (Author's collection)

In the 1950s, Garsdale's platform nameboards were marked 'For Hawes and Northallerton Line', as seen here with a train heading southbound on the Settle & Carlisle line. (Author's collection)

The Wensleydale Railway

'Dales line is reborn after nearly 50 years' said the *Independent* on 5th July 2003, referring to the previous day's first services on the Wensleydale Railway between Leeming Bar and Leyburn. This was only thirteen years after local residents had formed the Wensleydale Railway Association (WRA) with the aim of reinstating the railway through the dale. The trigger for this was the reprieve that year of the Settle–Carlisle line from a long-running closure proposal. When limestone shipments ended in December 1992, British Rail planned to lift the track between Northallerton and Redmire, but this threat was averted. The line was then used by the Ministry of Defence who invested £750,000 in retaining the rail link to Redmire for the movement of military vehicles to Catterick Camp. This allowed the Wensleydale Railway group to concentrate on securing the trackbed west of Redmire and the stations at Leeming Bar, Leyburn and Aysgarth. By October 2000 the WRA was ready to successfully launch Wensleydale Railway plc, which

The station at Leeming Bar was described as being 'the worse for wear' in 1989, but has now been refurbished by the Wensleydale Railway. (Author)

58

in spring 2003 took over the 22 mile track from Northallerton to Redmire on a 99 year lease and a few weeks later began its daily service using 'vintage' diesel multiple units.

In August 2004 the line in use for public services was extended by 4 miles to a temporary western terminus at Redmire, with an additional station reopened at Bedale. Further plans include restarting services east of Leeming to Northallerton, allowing an all-important connection with the East Coast Main Line. Eventually the railway hopes to reinstate services to Hawes, where the former station has been restored as a visitor centre and museum for the Yorkshire Dales. Part of the museum's displays are housed in three former railway coaches on a short length of track, which also has an ex-industrial 0-6-0 tank engine as a static exhibit. Perhaps one day the ultimate aim will be achieved – the restoration of rail services over the entire 40 miles between Northallerton and Garsdale. In November 2004 the railway began its first winter services, again running seven days a week, thus proving its commitment to transport in the valley, rather than being just another 'heritage railway'.

The first train of the new Wensleydale Railway arrives at Leyburn on 4th July 2003. (Wensleydale Railway plc)

6
Cleveland

Picton–Stokesley–Battersby
Middlesbrough to Guisborough
Guisborough to Saltburn and Loftus

Iron ore mining was the mainstay of the Cleveland railways for over a century. Here an ore train heads from Kilton mines into Lingthorpe Junction before closure in 1963. (Author's collection)

Picton–Stokesley–Battersby

The name 'Cleveland' was used in 1974 for the short-lived metropolitan county based on Middlesbrough and extending both sides of the River Tees. Historically Cleveland was south of the river and covered an area from the coast to the Esk valley, and beyond to the northernmost hills of the North York Moors. It

Map 4 Cleveland

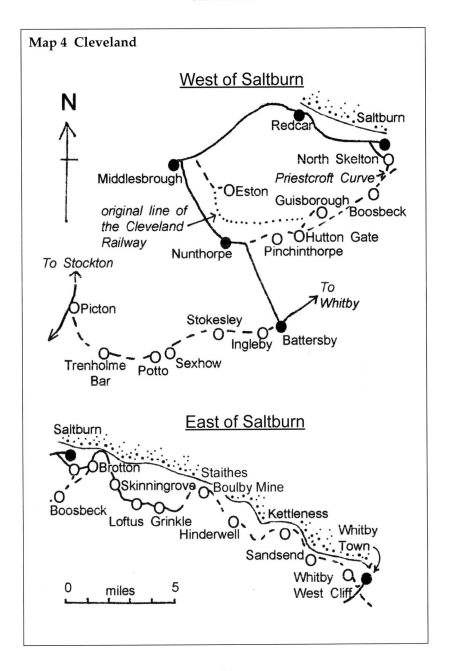

is the historical area that is dealt with here, entirely in Yorkshire and long important for the extraction of jet and alum, but it was iron ore mining that was the impetus for the area's railway development. First built was the Stockton & Darlington Railway's line to Middlesbrough (then called Port Darlington) in 1830, later extended to Redcar in 1846 and Saltburn in 1861. All these lines are still in use and the earliest line that has closed was a 12 mile stretch between Battersby and Picton, on the Leeds Northern's 1852 route from Northallerton to Stockton. Construction was by the North Yorkshire & Cleveland Railway (NY&C), and the line was opened from Picton to Stokesley in 1857, with intermediate stations at Trenholme Bar, Potto and Sexhow. Significantly, from Potto, a 2-mile branch led south to mines at Whorlton and there were soon two trains of ironstone daily from the branch and on to Picton and Stockton.

The NY&C's original Act in 1854 was for a railway right through from Picton to Grosmont on the Whitby & Pickering Railway (see Chapter 8). By the time the line was opened to Stokesley, a second Act provided for a link between Ingleby Junction, 3½ miles further and reached in 1858, and Nunthorpe Junction, to give easier access to Middlesbrough (for freight only at this stage). This and the line from Battersby to Grosmont, opened in stages to 1865, are the only sections of the NY&C scheme still in use and are part of Whitby's sole surviving rail link. A final NY&C Act in 1858 allowed for the takeover of the private narrow gauge railway to ironstone mines at Rosedale. Eventually this became a 19-mile standard gauge system, but only under the NER, which incorporated the NY&C in the Act of 1858. Thus it was the NER that completed the Stokesley–Ingleby Junction section for passenger use, with stations at Ingleby (village) and Ingleby Junction (renamed Battersby Junction in 1878 and Battersby from 1893).

The NER began services along the whole Esk valley in 1865 with four weekday trains each way between Whitby and Stockton. Freight trains were more numerous on the Picton–Battersby line, with six ironstone trains, a coke train for the ironworks at Grosmont and an ordinary goods train. The iron ore trade dwindled in the latter part of the 19th century; Grosmont ironworks closed in 1891 and the mines at Whorlton

Stokesley station in 1904. (J. Hodsdon, courtesy K.L. Taylor)

Stokesley station building today, well restored for use by a firm of architects. (Author)

Battersby station in 1957, with a Middlesbrough–Whitby train on the left. At the right is the line to Picton, used only for freight since 1954. (H. Davies)

the next year. Production at the Rosedale mines lingered until 1927 but the peak of 560,000 tons had been reached as early as 1873. With these shutdowns the line lost its importance for freight, but despite completion of the line along the coast in 1883, the Esk valley and Battersby–Picton lines remained a major passenger route between Whitby and Teesside, with seven weekday trains each way in 1900. However, by 1922 this was down to four, and by closure in 1954, only two. By then the westbound track from Ingleby to Picton was used for wagon storage only, requiring trains heading for Picton to reverse at Ingleby to get onto the eastbound track. Passenger services were withdrawn on 14th June 1954, and goods traffic ended west of Stokesley four years later, although the Stokesley–Battersby section stayed in use for freight until 1965. Since closure most of the line's stations have survived; Battersby is still operational for Whitby–Middlesbrough trains and the station buildings still stand at Ingleby, Stokesley, Sexhow and Potto, plus the stationmaster's house at Picton.

Middlesbrough to Guisborough

The small market town of Guisborough was the gateway to the richest area of iron ore mining in Cleveland; in 1910 the area's fifteen mines were producing fifty-five train loads each day. Mining was largely developed between 1850 and 1880, and this led to a boom in railway construction, starting with two rival schemes. First was the Middlesbrough & Guisborough Railway (M&G), backed by the major iron mine owners, the Pease family, which opened in 1853 to an iron ore mine at Cod Hill, with passenger services added the following year, These called at stations at Ormesby, Nunthorpe and Pinchinthorpe before a 'handsome little terminus' at Guisborough. There was a further station at Hutton Gate, which was exclusively for the use of the Pease family at nearby Hutton Hall.

The M&G had been promoted by the Stockton & Darlington Railway, which worked the line and absorbed it in 1858. By then

Pinchinthorpe has two surviving station buildings. This is the older one, built by the Middlesbrough & Guisborough Railway in 1854. (Author)

65

there was a potential rival for the lucrative iron ore trade. The West Hartlepool Harbour & Railway Company backed the Cleveland Railway, which that year obtained an Act for a line east of Guisborough, and its intention was also to build a line to the Tees in direct competition with the M&G. Three years of battles in Parliament and on the banks of the river ensued before an Act was finally agreed. By this time the Cleveland had largely built its line west of Guisborough anyway, using private schemes across its backers' estates, so it was able to run trains within five months of the Act. So by the end of 1861 there were two railways to Guisborough.

The situation was resolved by the NER, which absorbed the two rivals' parent companies in 1863–5. The Cleveland Railway was abandoned south of Ormesby, and a link put in from the line specified in its original Act east of Guisborough. This was to the former M&G line west of the town, leaving the station at the end of a short branch, so that trains between Middlesbrough and Loftus had to reverse at Guisborough until the end of those services in 1960. The NER also built a

The attractive station at Guisborough, seen here in 1955, has unfortunately not survived. (Stations UK)

Eston, on a spur from the former Cleveland Railway, was also a passenger terminus from 1902 to 1929, but its buildings were more like a collection of huts by 1955. (Stations UK)

new station at Pinchinthorpe, and in 1904 acquired Hutton Gate for public use from the Pease family. The remaining stretch of the former Cleveland Railway was connected to the Middlesbrough–Redcar line and run as a goods branch until 1966. The former M&G line is still operational to Nunthorpe Junction (as part of the Middlesbrough–Whitby service), but Pinchinthorpe closed in 1951, and Hutton Gate and Guisborough in 1964 when the branch line service to Middlesbrough ended. Little is left of the Cleveland line except for earthworks, best seen from the A171 west of Guisborough. The former M&G line has fared better; Hutton Gate and both Pinchinthorpe stations survive, with 3 miles of trackbed at the latter used as a public trail, but Guisborough station was lost to redevelopment in 1967.

Guisborough to Loftus and Saltburn

The Cleveland Railway's first Act in 1858 was for a line east of Guisborough to transport ironstone from the developing orefield. Progress was slow at first while the company concentrated on its battle for access to the Tees but by 1862 the railway had reached Boosbeck, then Brotton and Skinningrove in 1865. That year the Cleveland was absorbed by the NER, and it was left to that company to complete the line east to Loftus (Lofthouse until 1874) two years later. This involved the construction of Kilton Viaduct, with twelve stone piers carrying iron girders 150 ft above the Kilton Beck. The Cleveland's sole concern had been the iron ore trade, and no stations were built or passenger services run. This continued for the first ten years of NER ownership, despite the construction of a link to Saltburn in 1872, requiring a second major viaduct at Upleatham, this time with eleven arches and a total length of 783 ft. Eventually in 1875 stations were opened at Brotton, Skinningrove and Loftus, with a service to Saltburn. Three years later passenger services began between Loftus and Guisborough and, using the newly opened Priestcroft Curve, between Saltburn and Guisborough. A station was opened at Boosbeck in the same year (1878), and finally in 1902 one at North Skelton, south of Saltburn.

The completion of the coastal line east of Loftus in 1883, dealt with in the next chapter, allowed trains to run through between Whitby and Saltburn, giving a service of around six trains each way on weekdays in 1910. There were also passenger services from Middlesbrough and Guisborough; six to Saltburn (two via the Priestcroft Curve, four via Brotton) and two to Loftus. By 1911 ironstone mining had made Kilton Viaduct so unstable that the line had to be closed for two years and a 'charabanc' service provided for passengers between Skinningrove and Loftus. The viaduct was buried beneath 720,000 tons of spoil from local mine workings to create an embankment instead. In 1917 the Priestcroft Curve was taken out of use, requiring a reversal at Brotton for all services between Guisborough and Saltburn. As reversals were already required at both these places, with additional operating difficulties further along the coast at both

Brotton station in 1908. (K.L. Taylor collection)

The building is still recognisable today but has a different transport function! (Author)

Whitby and Scarborough, conventional steam trains were hardly appropriate. As early as 1905 the NER introduced its 'autocar', a small tank loco, with either one or two carriages each end of it and able to be driven from the outer end of a carriage. This was replaced in the 1920s by Sentinel steam railcars, including some of the larger 12 cylinder version, and in the 1930s a pioneer diesel electric railcar, *Tyneside Venturer*, was used. Around 1940 conventional steam locos equipped for push-pull working took over the services.

As detailed in the next chapter, from 1933 most trains ran between Loftus and Guisborough, leaving only a shuttle service between Brotton and Saltburn, which by 1949 was down to only two trains each way. North Skelton station closed in January 1951, but reopened for three summer months before closing permanently with the end of Brotton–Saltburn services in September, although the line continued to see some Scarborough–Middlesbrough summer services up to 1957. Skinningrove station was the next to close in 1952, but stayed in

Saltburn station was distinctive for its rail access to the adjacent Zetland Hotel, seen here in 1971 after the track had been lifted. (J.H. Meredith)

Waterfall Viaduct, with eight arches rising 60 ft, lies hidden in vegetation close to the A171. (Author)

The line east of Skinningrove was rebuilt in 1974, including this new viaduct at Carlin How being crossed by a potash train bound for Boulby in October 2003. (Author)

use for workers at the ironworks until 1958. Passenger trains east of Loftus ended in May 1958, and although diesel multiple units took over the Loftus–Guisborough service, this was unlikely to survive the loss of its coastal traffic. Closure to passengers (and goods west of Boosbeck) came in May 1960, with the Boosbeck–Brotton section closing to freight in September 1964. This was eight months after the shutdown of the area's last iron ore mine at North Skelton, which had produced over 25 million tons in its 92-year lifetime. The line from Saltburn through Brotton was retained to serve the ironworks at Skinningrove, and was still in place when the decision was taken to utilise it for the world's deepest potash mine at Boulby, opened in 1974. In 2003 there were eight potash trains each weekday, while the ironworks only used the line 'as required'. Of the area's former passenger stations, Brotton is still relatively intact, while stationmasters' houses remain at North Skelton and Boosbeck. Upleatham Viaduct is still used by the potash trains, while less easy to see is the disused Waterfall Viaduct east of Guisborough.

7
Coast Lines

Whitby to Loftus
Scarborough to Whitby
The Filey Holiday Camp branch

Loftus, shown here before closure in 1958, was the meeting point between lines east from Guisborough and west from Whitby. (Author's collection)

Whitby to Loftus

This line was considered to be one of the most scenic stretches of railway in the country, hugging the cliffs above the North Sea for the 10 miles from Whitby West Cliff to Staithes. It was built, at least initially, by the Whitby, Redcar & Middlesbrough Union Railway (WR&MU), which obtained its Act in 1866. Nothing was done until 1871, and a second Act was needed in 1873 to continue the work. In 1874 the contractor went into liquidation, and the following year the line was leased to the NER (and taken over in 1899). The NER found the previous work so unsatisfactory – bridges defective, piers out of vertical and tunnel surveys out of line – that much of it had to be done again. In particular part of the proposed line was so dangerously close to the cliff edge that the NER abandoned it and took a route further inland through Sandsend and Kettleness Tunnels. More problems were caused by the deep valleys dropping down to the sea, so that four viaducts were required on the stretch to Sandsend and a single large one at Staithes. All the bridges were tubular cast-iron frameworks filled with concrete, rather than the loose gravel the WR&MU had used at the start. Staithes Viaduct was still unfinished when the Tay Bridge disaster occurred, and had to be strengthened with extensive cross bracing. A wind gauge was also provided, although this proved

The viaduct at Staithes was the largest of the five on this stretch of line, 790 ft long with 17 spans soaring 150 ft above the Roxby Beck. (Author's collection)

Construction under way at the eastern entrance to Grinkle Tunnel in 1875. (Author's collection)

notoriously unreliable. These difficulties, plus Grinkle Tunnel towards Loftus, caused construction of the line to take as long as twelve years.

The first services were on 3rd December 1883, when the line opened without ceremony, but there were so many passengers for the first train at Whitby that extra carriages had to be provided, and many travelled without tickets. Stations had been built at Whitby West Cliff (convenient for the holiday resort area of the town), Sandsend, Kettleness, Hinderwell, Staithes and Easington (Grinkle from 1904), before an end-on junction with the former Cleveland Railway at Loftus station. The first services were from Whitby Town and Whitby West Cliff to Middlesbrough, but when the line from Scarborough was completed in 1885, these became Scarborough–Whitby West Cliff–Saltburn, with a reversal or shuttle service required for Whitby Town. Up to 1932 there were six weekday trains each way between Whitby and Loftus, but from the following year the line was described as 'deluged with passengers'! This was due to the introduction of cheap holiday Runabout Tickets and a change in the coastal services. The western destination reverted to Middlesbrough (via Guisborough), giving residents of Teesside much better access to Whitby and Scarborough. By the peak summer of 1939 there were thirteen trains each way every day, with two extras on Saturdays, plus reliefs and excursions. The line, a single track with passing loops at five of the stations, struggled to cope with the demand, but Grinkle station remained little used and closed in September 1939.

After 1945 the line saw intensive passenger activity again, but increasingly confined to summer weekends. In 1950 there were fourteen summer Saturday trains, usually of five coaches, and six trains on Sundays, but the winter service was down to three trains of two or three coaches on weekdays only. BR was thus

Class L1 2-6-4T no 67754 (which hauled the line's last scheduled northbound passenger train in 1958) is seen here at Staithes, with a camping coach at the left. (Author's collection)

able to claim in 1958 that £58,000 worth of maintenance was needed, mostly on the viaducts, for a line only fully used on a dozen summer Saturdays. Such services did not take place that year as closure (except for Whitby West Cliff – retained for the trains to Scarborough for another three years) came on 5th May 1958. Demolition started the next year, with the viaducts dismantled in 1960. They were sold for scrap with the concrete used for sea defences. Whitby West Cliff, Sandsend, Kettleness and Staithes station buildings survive, and a good impression of this coastal line can be gained by walking the trackbed for almost a mile from Sandsend village to the southern portal of Sandsend Tunnel.

Whitby's West Cliff station survives as 'Beechings Mews' – a questionable name as it closed two years before the infamous report was published. (Author)

Scarborough to Whitby

Whitby gained its first rail access in 1835 and Scarborough ten years later, but it took another forty years before there was a direct rail link between the two seaside towns. In the meantime there were five schemes, four Acts, and thirteen years of intermittent construction before the line finally opened on 16th July 1885. It had been built by the Scarborough & Whitby Railway Company, but was worked from the start by the NER for 50% of the gross profits. Eventually in 1897 the NER bought the line for £261,333, less than half the construction costs of almost £650,00 which included tunnels at Ravenscar and Falsgrave (Scarborough), a four-arch viaduct at Scalby and, most imposingly, the Larpool Viaduct over the Esk at Whitby. This was 915 ft long, 120 ft high, and its thirteen arches reputedly required over five million bricks. Initial services were four each way on weekdays only, calling at Scalby, Cloughton, Hayburn Wyke, Staintondale, Peak (Ravenscar from 1897), Fyling Hall, Robin Hood's Bay and Hawsker. There were operating difficulties at both ends; trains started at the south side of Scarborough station and then crossed the lines to and from York and Hull to the junction for the Whitby line. The loco then backed its train through Falsgrave Tunnel before running round it to get back to the front! At Whitby West Cliff a similar manoeuvre was needed for the train to get down to Whitby Town, although a shuttle service between the two was used for trains continuing to Saltburn. Difficulties were not confined to the ends as the line rose to a summit of 631 ft at Ravenscar. This posed most problems from the Whitby direction, involving almost 3 miles of climb at 1 in 39 on an exposed shelf overlooking Robin Hood's Bay, with a 279-yard-long tunnel almost at the summit. Sea fogs often left the rails wet and greasy, so that many times trains had to reverse for another try. Summer excursions from Whitby were often double-headed, five coaches being the limit for one engine, and as late as 19th January 1959, both steam locos and diesel multiple units failed to make any progress for much of the day. The line was also badly affected by snow, being blocked in the winter of 1885/6, and for two weeks in 1947.

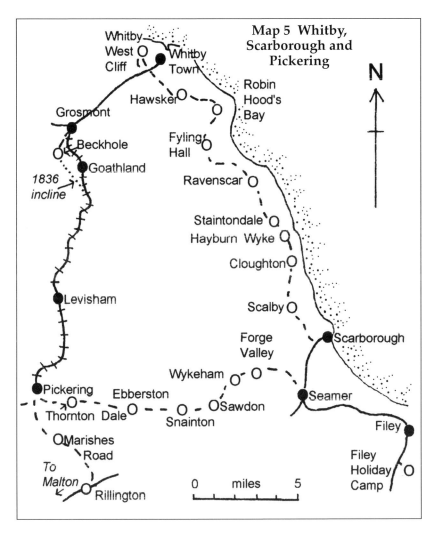

Map 5 Whitby, Scarborough and Pickering

Services increased steadily to summer 1932, when there were seven weekday trains and three on Sundays. As on the Whitby–Loftus line, the changes in 1933 led to a major expansion and alterations in working practice, notably at Scarborough station. An extra platform, 1A, was cut out of the far end of the northernmost platform, which allowed summer trains to back out past the junction and then set off for Whitby. The downside

From 1934 Whitby trains departed from their own platform at Scarborough, seen here with Fairburn class 4P no 42083. (D.L. Chatfield)

was the lengthy walk along platform 1 for passengers laden with holiday luggage; it is said that trains left three minutes later than the advertised time to allow for this! By July 1938 there were fifteen trains each way, with three extra on Saturdays and thirteen on Sundays, but after the closure of the line to Loftus in 1958, winter services were down to four trains on weekdays with none on Sundays. The first closure came with Scalby station in 1953, although certain summer Saturday trains continued to call for holidaymakers using the camping coaches there. These had been introduced by the LNER in 1933, and proved so popular that by 1938 there were ten at stations on this line. After World War II, BR revived the scheme, and by 1963 the four coaches at Scalby were part of the line's allocation of sixteen, but 1964 was the last year the scheme operated in this region. It was also the end for goods trains on the Scarborough–Whitby line (14th August), with passenger services finishing on 6th March 1965. The last train was watched by crowds at the stations, including 91 year old Fred Meynell at Robin Hood's Bay; eighty years earlier as a schoolboy he had cheered the first train on the line.

Larpool Viaduct over the River Esk is arguably the most magnificent survival from the railway age in North and East Yorkshire. (J. Suggitt)

A more modest but still fine survivor is Staintondale station – with its clock still keeping good time. (Author)

George Andrews designed Scarborough station in 1845, although the clock tower was added forty years later; the whole station is much altered since this 1968 view. (J.H. Meredith)

Attempts were made to use the line for preservation schemes in both 1966 and 1967, but these failed. The track from Hawsker to Whitby was at first left for a proposed potash mine (that was built at Boulby instead), but by 1985 Scarborough Borough Council was able to complete a 'railway path' on almost the entire length of the former line. This provides an outstanding 23 mile walk which includes the Scalby Viaduct and half of the original eight station buildings. The highlight, however, is the Larpool Viaduct, which can be also be viewed from the unofficial path following the former link down towards Whitby Town station.

The Filey Holiday Camp branch

A short branch 11½ miles from Scarborough (by rail) will be remembered by thousands who used it to get to their holiday destination. The cliffs south of Filey were the location for the third Butlins holiday camp, begun before the Second World War

The lengthy platforms at the terminus, with few passengers from the arrival of diesel multiple units in 1977, the last year of operation. (Author's collection)

The deserted and overgrown scene in 2003. (C. Skelton)

but not open to holidaymakers until 1945. The following year a ½ mile rail link to the Filey–Bridlington line of 1847 came into use, though it was not officially opened until May 10th 1947. A North Curve and South Curve (with signal box) led to two huge uncovered 500 ft long platforms, each with lines on either side, with an extra track in the middle (later removed) allowing locos to change ends of the trains. Beyond ticket barriers was a basic terminal building at the end of a subway, through which a garishly painted 'road-train' took holidaymakers under the busy A165 and into the camp.

The camp expanded to be the largest in the Butlins 'empire' by the late 1960s, with a capacity of 11,000. By 1952 its railway branch was already used by summer Saturday trains from as far away as Worcester and London King's Cross. Works and society excursions were also popular, such as the centenary trip in 1964 for staff at Broadbents, a Huddersfield engineering firm. In the late 60s and early 70s, the branch became a mecca for train enthusiasts as ex-LNER Pacifics including the *Flying Scotsman* regularly reversed to the 'Butlins Triangle' to turn there, due to the lack of a turntable big enough for them at Scarborough. However, by the late 70s, the growth of road transport to the camp meant the line was little used and its last trains ran on 17th September 1977. Six years later with changes in holiday patterns the camp itself shut down, and now little is to be seen of either the camp or its rail link.

8
Across the North York Moors

Grosmont–Pickering–Malton
The North Yorkshire Moors Railway

Steam age scene? Perhaps the clothing shows this is modern-day Grosmont with the North Yorkshire Moors Railway's ex-BR Standard class 4 2-6-0 no 76079. (Mrs R. Gibbons)

Grosmont–Pickering–Malton

South of the River Esk, the Cleveland Hills merge into an upland area known as the North York Moors, which has given its name to a National Park. It is crossed by several river valleys aligned north–south, and despite various schemes, only one of these ever saw a railway line – Newtondale, the easternmost and narrowest valley. Its line was built by the Whitby & Pickering Railway (W&P), engineered by George Stephenson and completed as early as 1836. Unusually, even for that time, it used horse-drawn carriages throughout. The route followed the River Esk from Whitby to Grosmont, crossing the river nine times on wooden bridges, and with stops at Ruswarp and Sleights. After a short tunnel at Grosmont, the valley of the Murk Esk was used as far as Beckhole. The horses were detached here, and a self-balancing rope-worked incline was used to haul the carriages for 1,500 yards up to Goathland (Bank Top). Horses then took over again for a gentler climb to the summit level of over 500 ft at Fen Bog and the lengthy descent of Newtondale, with a stop at Levisham, to Pickering, although for the steepest part gravity alone was used.

Services began between Whitby and Grosmont in 1835, with the formal opening through to Pickering on 26th May 1836. There were usually two daily trains each way, except Sundays,

The castellated entrance to what has been described as the world's earliest railway tunnel, at Grosmont. (Author)

This cottage at Goathland is believed to have been the waiting room at the top of the incline from Beckhole. (Author)

taking almost 2½ hours for the 24 mile journey, with a stagecoach connection at Pickering for York. Despite its primitive operating methods, the line was a success both for passengers and freight, especially ironstone mined near Grosmont and sent out through Whitby. However, finances were a major problem, its construction cost having reached £105,060 rather than the estimated £48,000. In 1845 it was bought by the York & North Midland Railway (Y&NM), which in the same year reached Pickering using a branch from its York–Scarborough route at Rillington, with an intermediate station at Marishes Road. The Y&NM rebuilt the W&P route with double track to take steam locomotives, which were introduced in July 1847. A new tunnel at Grosmont was needed but the incline remained in use, though worked by a stationary steam engine.

It was not until 1865 that the incline was replaced. The NER, formed from the Y&NM and other companies in 1854, built a 4½ mile deviation line from south of Grosmont to the summit at Fen

Bog. The halts at Beckhole and Bank Top were also replaced by a single station at Goathland Mill (Goathland from 1891). However, the original line north from the incline foot to Grosmont remained intact, and between 1908 and 1914 there was even a summer-only passenger service from Whitby to Beckhole, where a simple wooden station was built. Occasional goods services continued as far as the isolated hamlet of Esk Valley until 1951 when a road was built. The year 1933 provides a 'snapshot' of movements on the line, with a basic service of five trains each way between Whitby and Malton, with two extra in summer, and a much increased service of 9–10 trains on Saturdays, including some to and from York, a through carriage for London King's Cross, and a summer-only additional service between Whitby and Goathland. This also ran on summer Sundays when the line saw double-headed 'Scenic Excursion' trains from West Yorkshire, which ran out by this line and returned by the coast line to Scarborough.

Services remained much the same under BR, and by 1962

One of the 1950s 'Scenic Excursions' approaches Goathland Summit with class 2MT 2-6-2T 41265 heading a class B1 from West Yorkshire. (P. Wilson)

A precursor of the line's preservation: Class K4 2-6-0 no 3442 'The Great Marquess' with a three-coach special for a television programme at Goathland in 1964. (G. Hardy)

most trains were diesel multiple units, which were packed on summer weekends. Thus it came as a shock when the Beeching Report suggested that all three remaining lines to Whitby should close to passengers. There was a massive protest with a record number of formal objections, which resulted in the retention of the line to Battersby, rather than the route through Pickering, which had been regarded as Whitby's 'premier' rail access. Closure to passengers south of Grosmont came on 6th March 1965, although the Rillington–Pickering section was retained for goods for another sixteen months. Grosmont to Whitby remains in use as part of the Whitby–Middlesbrough service, while the North Yorkshire Moors Railway has revived trains between Grosmont and Pickering (see next section). Only Pickering–Rillington and the original line at Goathland count as 'lost' railways, with the latter now a footpath. It is the former incline that provides most interest as the route is still intact and gives a good impression of an early railway.

The North Yorkshire Moors Railway

Local councils had tried unsuccessfully to reopen the Pickering–Grosmont line since closure in 1965. On 3rd June 1967 a group of local people set up the North Yorkshire Moors Railway Preservation Society to take over the fight. As there were soon rumours that BR was about to lift the tracks, an agreement was reached deferring such work. In 1969 the society, now a company, bought the land, buildings and one line of track between Grosmont and the summit, plus the railway land and buildings to High Mill, Pickering. Maintenance work on the purchased section began in November 1968, with steam gala weekends commencing in 1970. BR then proceeded to lift the second track between stations. The work done by 1971 was sufficient to convince the County Council that the scheme was viable and help was provided for the purchase of the remaining track. Just over eight years after closure, the whole line from Grosmont to Pickering reopened to public services on 22nd April 1973.

Rolling stock from the early days of preservation – 0-6-0ST no 47 'Moorbarrow' and an ex-BR diesel unit at Pickering station in the 1970s. (Author's collection)

For two years the Pickering terminus had to be at High Mill, as the station was under threat of demolition for a supermarket and car park. This was averted following a public inquiry and the station was restored to railway use, although what was probably the original 1836 building was lost. However, the stations at Levisham and Grosmont remain intact, although the latter has a new signal box by the level crossing. Goathland is a particularly fine example of a NER country station, and a more workaday halt for walkers at Newtondale has been well used since opening in 1981. In 1973 the railway began with diesel services over the whole line at weekends between April and October, with steam trains between Grosmont and Goathland on similar dates plus up to four weekdays in mid-summer.

Over thirty years later the service is now almost year-round, though restricted to weekends in November and December, and school holidays January to March. For much of the summer

By 1992 heavier traction was in use, including this Austerity class 2-10-0 no 3672, renamed 'Dame Vera Lynn', seen with a fine view of Goathland station. (J. Suggitt)

The present-day scene is represented here by ex-BR Standard class 4 no 76079, awaiting departure from Grosmont in October 2003. (Author)

holiday period as many as eight return journeys a day are made over the whole line. Except for an annual Diesel Gala and some journeys at other times, all trains are now scheduled for steam haulage. Special events include weekends for 'Friends of Thomas the Tank Engine', vintage vehicles, and recollections of World War II, along with Santa Specials. Dining Trains run throughout the year. In the foreseeable future the railway hopes to operate further occasional trains to and from Whitby, while the County Council's long-term policy is to rebuild the line between Pickering and Rillington Junction, on the York–Scarborough line. Helped by its setting amidst the scenery of the North York Moors National Park, plus its use in many films and television programmes, the line can justifiably claim to be the country's most popular heritage railway.

9
The Vale of Pickering

The Forge Valley Line
Pilmoor–Gilling–Malton
Gilling–Pickering

In the 1950s and early 1960s, class V2 2-6-2 locomotives such as no 60948 were regularly seen in the area on trips to Ampleforth College and the coast. (Author's collection)

The Forge Valley Line

To the south of the upland area of the North York Moors lies a low flat plain, the western part of which is called 'Ryedale' (the name used by the local district council), and the eastern part 'The Carrs'. The older term 'Vale of Pickering' covers the whole area. Stretching some 35 miles west–east it is extremely flat in places, suggesting its origins as a former lake floor, and is subject to extensive flooding. Railways kept to its edges, with the last to be built hugging its north-east corner. This was the Seamer and

93

Pickering branch, more commonly called the Forge Valley Line, built and opened by the NER in 1882. It should not be confused with proposals for a Forge Valley Railway, using the narrow valley north from East and West Ayton. This would have linked with the Scarborough–Whitby line, and got as far as a Bill for Parliament in 1873 but was withdrawn. The Forge Valley Line ran for 16¼ miles of single track from Seamer Junction, 3 miles south of Scarborough on the former York & North Midland route to Malton and York, to just south of Pickering, where it joined the same company's line from Rillington.

Intermediate stations were built at Forge Valley (serving East and West Ayton), Wykeham, Sawdon, Snainton, Ebberston (Wilton until 1903) and Thornton Dale. Services were four weekday trains each way; there was never a Sunday service and few excursions except for some to and from Helmsley. In 1928 the line became the first in the area with a regular Sentinel steam railcar service for passengers, which continued for the next twenty years. The Sentinels were mechanically unreliable, and struggled to cope with attachments such as horseboxes,

An early 1950s scene at Pickering station, with Malton-based class J25 0-6-0 no 65723 on goods duty. (P. Wilson)

94

Sawdon station, serving the village of Brompton, has now been restored as holiday accommodation. (Author)

Forge Valley station also survives, but in more workaday use as a council highways depot! (Author)

commonly required in such a rural backwater. All the stations except Wykeham had facilities to deal with livestock, and such agricultural produce comprised most of the freight on the line, although there was also stone from a quarry at Thornton Dale. This kept the western 3 miles of the line open until 1964, after passenger services (and the rest of the freight) had ended on Saturday 3rd June 1950. The last passenger train was the 6.40 pm from Scarborough with two coaches for Pickering, hauled by ex-LNER class G5 0-4-4T no 67273. Unusually all six of the line's former station buildings survive, the highlight probably being Ebberston, which was restored in 1998 with a section of track and three ex-British Rail coaches converted to holiday accommodation – a 21st century equivalent of the LNER's camping coaches at Thornton Dale and Forge Valley.

Pilmoor–Gilling–Malton

Access to the vale from the west was from the present-day East Coast Main Line at Pilmoor. Three schemes were proposed in 1845, and it was the Newcastle & Darlington Junction Railway's Thirsk & Malton branch that gained Parliamentary approval. The company changed name three times before the line opened

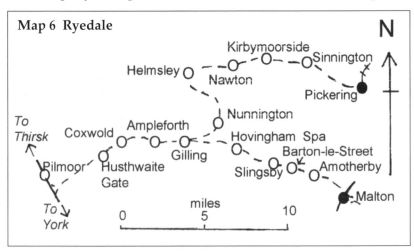

Map 6 Ryedale

in 1853, and the following year became part of the NER. There were also changes to the original plans, but the line was built to run from a north–east curve at Pilmoor for 23 miles to Scarborough Road Junction at Malton. The original plan was for a junction with the York–Scarborough line, but instead it joined the Malton & Driffield Junction Railway, whose tracks could be used into Malton station. The opening day, 19th May 1853, was a combined occasion for both lines with a twelve-coach train travelling from Malton to Pilmoor, then back through Malton to Driffield and finally back to Malton for a 'sumptuous repast'.

The line's initial passenger services were between Thirsk and Malton, and in 1856 there was one train shuttling to and fro three times a day. Intermediate stations had been provided at Husthwaite Gate, Coxwold, Ampleforth, Gilling, Hovingham (which added 'Spa' in 1896), Slingsby, Barton-le-Street and Amotherby. When the Gilling & Pickering line was completed in 1875, there were trains through to York using the southbound Pilmoor Curve to Bishophouse Junction, but only from the Pickering branch and covering the westernmost 12 miles of this line. By 1895 there were four such trains daily, and the line to

Gilling station, seen here in 1926, was the point at which the lines split, the left hand signals marking the line to Pickering, those on the right the line to Malton. (Stations UK)

Slingsby station around 1910. This is one of the few stations on this line that has survived. (Stations UK)

Malton was already the 'poor relation'. Its trains to Thirsk ended by 1914, and nine years later it was only a feeder for the York–Pickering service, and even this function ended on 30th December 1930, when the four easternmost stations closed. The western end kept its local passenger services (except at Ampleforth station, which closed in 1950) until the York–Pickering trains ended in 1953.

The line did have two quite different sets of 'main line' workings. The boys' boarding school of Ampleforth College is situated between Ampleforth and Gilling stations. From the 1930s up to 1964 there were two special 'school trains' at the beginning and end of each term, usually to and from London King's Cross and Leeds or Liverpool, with one to summer camp at the end of July. These regularly provided the unusual sight of an ex-LNER Pacific along the line to Gilling, although after 1953 this brought the College special to Malton instead, where a local engine took over. Between 1932–1939 and 1947–1962, the line also saw summer Saturday holiday trains to and from Scarborough. The LNER began these to avoid the congestion at

The last workings over the whole line were Scarborough summer specials, including this relief train to Darlington with class B1 4-6-0 no 61224, seen west of Malton. (Author's collection)

York, running two trains in each direction, despite the need for a double reversal at Malton. This was achieved by the Malton pilot engine pulling the train, with its loco at the other end, between Scarborough Road Junction and Malton station. Filey Holiday Camp trains avoided this for three summers after 1947 as they carried on to the Malton & Driffield line – a rare case of the two lines used together for passenger workings. In summer 1959 there were four scheduled Saturday workings to and from Scarborough, but these did not run after 1962. The northbound junction with the East Coast Main Line was not replaced after an accident in March 1963 and so the Thirsk & Malton line lost its last through passenger trains. Goods traffic ended on 7th August 1964, except for 3½ miles at Malton, which closed ten weeks later.

Gilling–Pickering

Two of the 1845 schemes for the western part of the vale included branches to the small towns on its northern edge – Helmsley and Kirkbymoorside – but these were not built. Nor was the planned Ryedale Railway of 1862, although its route linking the two towns to Pickering and the Thirsk & Malton line was similar to that eventually built by the NER. That company's original Act for the branch in 1866 was designed to oppose a rival scheme through Helmsley that would have linked Leeds to Teesside. Once that was defeated, the NER proceeded slowly, even trying to back out of the project in 1868. However, by 1871 it had opened a southern curve at Pilmoor and the new branch as far as Helmsley, which was extended to Kirkbymoorside (the station name used by the railways was 'Kirbymoorside' – without the second 'k') three years later and finally through to Pickering in 1875. Additional stations were provided at Nunnington, Nawton and Sinnington, with initial services

The last Gilling-Pickering passenger services were handled by locos from Shire and Hunt class D49 including no 62749 'The Cottesmore'. (Author's collection)

Helmsley station, still with its glass verandah in 1957, and a Branch Line Society railtour. (Stations UK)

Kirbymoorside station buildings, along with Nunnington and Nawton, survive and are still in use. (J. Suggitt)

mostly as far as Gilling to link with the Thirsk & Malton trains. Gradually the Gilling & Pickering became the dominant line, with trains through to York replacing those from Malton to Thirsk by 1914. Generally there were two to four such trains each way on weekdays, right up to closure on 31st January 1953, a date more associated with the North Sea floods in Eastern England and Holland. The last train was the 6 pm York–Pickering hauled by D49 4-4-0 'Shire' class no 62735 *Westmorland*. The only passenger trains after that were trips including Ramblers' Excursions to Kirkbymoorside from West Yorkshire, the last of which, quaintly titled 'Special Ramblers' Daffodil and Primrose Diesel Excursion', ran on 3rd May 1964. In the early 1960s there were also special trains out from the area, chiefly from Helmsley as far as Largs, London and King's Lynn, and more modest Sunday School outings to Scarborough. The last of these ran on 27th July 1964, and two weeks later the line closed altogether.

10
Over the Yorkshire Wolds

Malton to Driffield
York–Market Weighton–Beverley
Selby–Market Weighton–Driffield

Class B16 4-6-0 locos were often used on workings to and from the coast; here no 61432 heads over the Wolds at Enthorpe. (Author's collection)

Malton to Driffield

As well as the three major companies involved in the formation of the NER in 1854, there was a 20 mile branch line – the Malton & Driffield Junction Railway (M&D). In 1845 its original title had been the Newcastle-upon-Tyne & Hull Direct Railway, but the more realistic name was soon adopted instead. Its proposed layout was hardly suited to long-distance traffic, as its junctions at both ends faced away from Newcastle and Hull respectively. However, it was backed by George Hudson, along with the

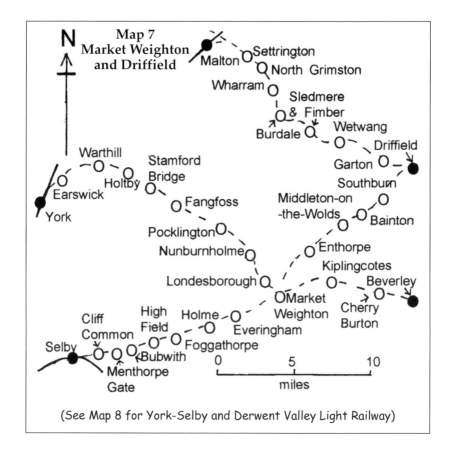

(See Map 8 for York-Selby and Derwent Valley Light Railway)

Thirsk & Malton (T&M), which would meet it at Malton's Scarborough Road Junction. The Act for the line was passed in 1846 and engineers appointed. Although the consulting engineer was John Birkinshaw, his on-site assistant was Alfred Dickens, younger brother of the famous Victorian writer. When asked in Parliament if there would be any engineering difficulties, Alfred had replied 'none whatever', a claim that must have haunted him over the next seven years as such problems surely contributed to his early death in 1860.

The construction difficulties came with the Yorkshire Wolds, a line of chalk hills across the path of the proposed line. Although not particularly high, they formed a barrier which the company decided to tackle with the 1,606 yard Burdale Tunnel (extended during construction to 1,744 yards). Work began in spring 1847, but by August 1848 only 150 yards of tunnel had been dug. The problems were not so much physical as financial; Hudson's railway empire was collapsing, and the M&D was struggling to get its own line built and also needed completion of the T&M, without which it would lose the possibility of a through route on towards Newcastle. By 1849 the company was on the verge of bankruptcy, and work on the line was at a standstill. Somehow the project survived, helped by a decision to build it as a single line rather than the over-optimistic double track of the proposals. Work resumed in 1850, and although a new Act was required in 1851 to allow completion, this was achieved in 1853. The finished project hardly looked like a main line, particularly the stations at Settrington, North Grimston, Wharram, Burdale, Fimber (Sledmere & Fimber from 1858), Wetwang and Garton, which were built by local contractors and looked like farmhouses with few facilities and platforms barely 18 inches high.

The line's opening ceremony was shared with the T&M on 19th May 1853, but the Board of Trade would not allow public

Settrington station in the 1920s showing the low original platform and well-tended gardens. (Lens of Sutton Association)

105

The former Sledmere & Fimber station building in 1969, nineteen years after closure (it was later demolished). (Author's collection)

All that survives at the Sledmere & Fimber station site is this well-hidden former crossing keeper's cottage. (Author)

services until 1st June. Initial passenger services were three trains each way on weekdays, which remained the pattern for the 'Malton Dodger' over the next 97 years. Little changed on this line, described as 'the most truly rural branch on the NER', although there were royal visits to Sledmere & Fimber, holiday trains for Butlins at Filey between 1947 and 1950, and scenic excursions from Hull even after the end of scheduled passenger services on 3rd June 1950. These were possible as the line was kept open for shipments from huge chalk quarries at Wharram (1918–1930) and Burdale (1922–1955). In the 1920s over 100,000 tons of chalk a year were sent to steelworks on Teesside via the former T&M – a rare example of the long-distance traffic envisaged by the M&D's promoters. When this ended in 1955 there was no need to keep the line open, and it closed finally in October 1958. Most of its stations survive except for Burdale and Sledmere & Fimber, and the line can be walked at Wharram past the chalk silo left from the line's quarrying days.

An imposing water tank is among the railway survivals at the former Wharram station. (Author)

York–Market Weighton–Beverley

The central section of the Yorkshire Wolds south of Driffield was crossed by two remarkably similar railways. Both were begun by the York & North Midland (Y&NM) and completed by the NER. Unlike the Malton & Driffield further north and the Hull & Barnsley to the south, both avoided tunnelling through the hills. The two lines met at the small town of Market Weighton and both closed in 1965, although their opening dates differed by ten months. First was the York–Market Weighton line, built across the Vale of York with few construction difficulties, although 22 level crossings were required. It opened on 3rd October 1847, with three trains each way daily (except Sundays). There were intermediate stations at Huntington (Earswick), Stockton (Warthill), Stamford Bridge, Fangfoss, Pocklington, Burnby (Nunburnholme) and Shipton (Londesborough). The names in brackets are those used by the NER, which continued the changes with the Y&NM's additional station of Gate Helmsley (1848), renamed Holtby. A private halt was also provided for George Hudson at Londesborough Hall, which went out of use after his downfall. The principal stations were at Pocklington and Market Weighton, both with overall roofs, imposing frontages and extensive facilities.

Although an extension east across the Wolds to Beverley was in the line's Act of 1846, no progress was made with this, largely due to the opposition of a prominent local landowner, Lord Hotham. Completion was left to the NER, formed from the Y&NM and other companies in 1854. At first it considered a line south-east to Brough instead, but by 1860 was committed to the original scheme. A new Act was obtained in June 1862, and construction began later that year. Even then his Lordship successfully opposed a station at Goodmanham in favour of one at Kiplingcotes, and insisted on no Sunday trains. These never did run (except for a few diversions), although the NER was not keen on them anyway! The line eventually opened on 1st May 1865, with an increased service of four York–Hull trains daily, and one other intermediate station at Cherry Burton.

For the next hundred years the line continued as a secondary

A York–Hull train headed by class B1 no 61010 'Wildebeeste' calls for anglers at Stamford Bridge in the late 1950s. (D.P. Leckonby)

link between York and Hull, with summer weekend trains to the coast. Scheduled services reached a peak of nine weekday trains each way as late as 1960. By then most trains were DMUs, and several intermediate stations had closed. First to shut was Holtby, for passengers in 1939 and freight in 1951, when Nunburnholme also closed. Warthill, Fangfoss and Cherry Burton shut to passengers eight years later, and Kiplingcotes became an unstaffed halt. The line's prospects looked good in 1960 when a modernisation scheme was announced, including single line working and the installation of colour light signalling. This would have cost £83,036 and was approved by BR, so it came as a complete shock when the line was listed for closure in the Beeching Report. Despite a vigorous campaign and a seven week reprieve, the line shut completely on 29th November 1965. Most of the trackbed west of Market Weighton has returned to farmland, but Stamford Bridge Viaduct was saved and can be walked, together with over ½ mile of trackbed. A much lengthier walk is available between Market Weighton and Beverley, where a 10 mile stretch of trackbed has been made into a path named the Hudson Way.

East Yorkshire's only substantial viaduct, shown here in 1971 but still standing, took the York–Market Weighton line over the River Derwent at Stamford Bridge. (J.H. Meredith)

110

Pocklington station, seen here disused in 1974, is an outstanding example of the reuse of railway premises as it has been restored as a sports hall for Pocklington School. (J.H. Meredith)

The former Kiplingcotes station is also well preserved; in addition to the platform, nameboard and goods shed shown here, the station building and signal box also survive. (Author)

Most stations survive, including Pocklington with its fine frontage and overall roof. The other major station, Market Weighton, was demolished but the next station to the north-west, Londesborough, was still lived in by ex-railwayman Syd Walker and his wife in May 2004. Syd had worked on the railways for 42 years until his retirement in 1980, chiefly as a signalman. Among the closed stations featured in this book, his career had included stints at Ravenscar, Newton Kyme, Sledmere & Fimber (where Mrs Walker operated the crossing gates) and Bainton, as well as Londesborough. The programme 'Off the Rails' in the BBC's *Nation on Film* series shown in 2003 included Syd remembering the last day of services at Market Weighton, Saturday 27th November 1965, when the station had a wreath provided by the staff. It also showed footage of him in Market Weighton West signal box in 1965, and featured him as the only survivor of the Market Weighton station staff from that time. The Walkers' home since 1966, Londesborough station

Ex-railwayman Syd Walker at his home, the former Londesborough station house, in May 2004. (Author)

building has many of its original doors and windows, and its brickwork still features bricks stamped 'WW' and '1847' indicating the builder (William Watson) and construction date.

Selby–Market Weighton–Driffield

This line too was built in stages, with the opening of the western section preceding that to the east by almost 42 years! Construction of the Selby–Market Weighton part was easy across the level Vale of York, with only one major obstacle, the River Derwent, crossed by a wood and cast-iron viaduct. Much of the line followed a dead straight course, and it is surprising that its opening by the Y&NM was delayed until 1st August 1848. This may have been due to disputes over station sites, and the only intermediate stations ready for the opening appear to have been Bubwith and Holme (Holme Moor from 1923). The Y&NM added others at Cliff Common Gate, Duffield Gate (which was soon closed), Menthorpe Gate, Foggathorpe Gate and Harswell Gate. The NER dropped the suffix 'Gate', except at Menthorpe Gate, changed Harswell Gate to Everingham, and added another station at Bubwith High Field (High Field from 1873).

Initial services were two weekday trains each way between Selby and Market Weighton, and the line remained a rural backwater pending the extension through to Driffield. The NER was in no hurry to complete this, and was only spurred into action by a rival scheme in 1884. This was put forward by the Scarborough, Bridlington & West Riding Junction Railway (SB&WRJ), and would have linked Scarborough to Howden. Much of its route was never a practicable proposition, and three years later the scheme was reduced to a Market Weighton–Driffield link. This was built by the SB&WRJ, which remained nominally independent until 1913, though its services were operated from the start by the NER. The line climbed from Market Weighton for 3½ miles at 1 in 100 up Enthorpe Bank to the isolated Enthorpe station, before a long descent through stations at Middleton-on-the-Wolds, Bainton and Southburn to

The climb to the mile-long cutting at Enthorpe often required double-heading; in this case, by Hunt class D49 no 62775 and class 4MT no 43125 on a Scarborough–Liverpool working in 1958. (Author's collection)

Driffield. Passenger services began on 1st May 1890 with three daily trains each way, and by 1902 included a Bridlington–Leeds through train both ways.

After World War II, it was summer Saturday trains to the coast that kept the line in use. On Saturday 9th August 1952, for example, there were fifteen scheduled trains over the line heading for Bridlington, Filey Holiday Camp and Scarborough, plus another fifteen excursions. However, local traffic was almost non-existent, and ended in September 1954 with the closure of all intermediate stations to passengers except Market Weighton (Menthorpe Gate had already shut in 1953). By the 1960s there were only two weekday passenger trains between Selby and Driffield and one in the opposite direction, and it was clear that these, along with the reduced holiday workings, could all be diverted via Hull. Thus the end as a through route came on 14th June 1965, before the start of the summer season, though freight lingered on the Selby–Market Weighton section until August. Most station buildings survive west of Market

A passenger working for the coast heads through Enthorpe station, disused after 1959. (Author's collection)

The hedge at the former Holme Moor station has NER memorabilia, including this distinctive ¼ mile post. (Author)

Weighton, but only Bainton to the east. In addition a 9-mile stretch of the former trackbed is walkable as the Bubwith Trail. This begins with a nature reserve just to the east of the remains of the viaduct over the Derwent (rebuilt by the NER in 1858), and ends at the A614 west of Market Weighton.

11
Around Selby

Selby to York
The Cawood branch
Selby to Goole
The Derwent Valley Light Railway

Selby in the 1950s, with A1 Pacific no 60129 'Guy Mannering' hauling a southbound express on the East Coast Main Line. (R.S. Carpenter)

Selby to York

Most 'lost railways' were formerly secondary lines or branches, rather than main lines, so it is particularly unusual to have a stretch that was once part of the East Coast Main Line (ECML). When a major coalfield was developed west of the town of Selby in the 1970s, the route used by London King's Cross–Edinburgh

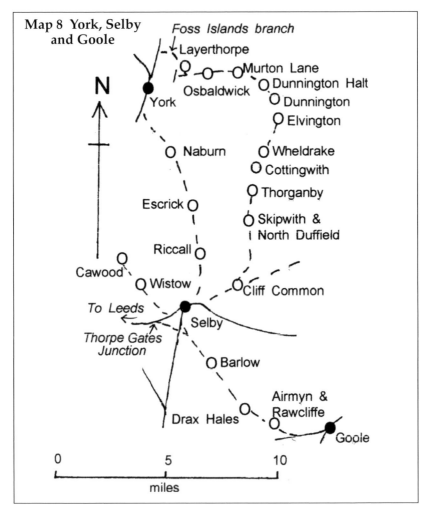

Map 8 York, Selby and Goole

trains for the previous hundred years became liable to subsidence. A 14½ mile replacement line was built further west at a cost of £60 million, and the old route north of Selby was abandoned. This had been quite a late addition to the ECML, as George Hudson had ensured that the first line to York was his York & North Midland Railway, completed in 1840 from the Derby–Leeds line at Normanton. This circuitous route from

London was somewhat shortened by a link from the GNR at Knottingley, opened in 1850, but it was another twenty-one years before a direct connection from Doncaster to York via Selby was completed. The NER's Act had been passed in 1864, but financial problems delayed the line's opening until 1871.

The 1871 line ran from Shaftholme Junction, north of Doncaster, through four minor stations to Selby, where it used ½ mile of the Hull & Selby Railway (1840) including a crossing of the River Ouse. From Barlby Junction a further additional stretch of track headed through stations at Riccall, Escrick and Naburn, where the Ouse was crossed again, to Chaloner Whin Junction outside York. Once York's present-day station was opened in 1877, the route became available for high speed running and featured in the 'railway races' of 1888 and 1895, and the LNER record-breaking runs of the 1930s. Amidst all this the line north of Selby did have a local service; in 1910 for example there were eight stopping trains daily to York (one on Sundays). Such trains hardly fitted in with the Anglo-Scottish expresses, and Naburn

The line also saw much freight traffic, represented here by class 47 diesel-electric no 1998 on a 'merry-go-round' coal working at Barlby in 1972. (J.H. Meredith)

and Escrick stations closed to passengers in 1953, followed by Riccall five years later. Selby kept its status as a stopping point for at least some north–south trains; in the 1970s eighteen northbound trains called there, and sixteen southbound. The diversion of the ECML due to the coalfield development was completed in 1983; York–Hull services began using it in May, while the express trains transferred on 3rd October when the old line closed north of Selby.

South of the town the former ECML is still in use for local services to Doncaster. To the north, the first 3½ miles were used for a new road bypass for Barlby and Riccall, but then 7 miles are available to walkers and cyclists as the York & Selby Railway Path. This passes the sites of Escrick station, with no remains, and Naburn where the station house survives. Also at Naburn the path crosses the former swing bridge over the Ouse, now without its control turret and signal box, but boasting a sculpture instead.

The former swing bridge at Naburn survives and is part of the 'York & Selby Railway Path'. (Author)

The Cawood branch

Selby has not only lost its north–south main line but two branches to Cawood and Goole as well. Schemes to link the villages of Cawood and Wistow to Selby were promoted as early as 1879, including one for the grandly-titled 'Selby & Mid-Yorkshire Union Railway'. By the early 1890s the proposal was reduced to a more modest Cawood & Wistow Light Railway, although the Light Railways Act was not yet in force and this was just the name chosen. Operating plans were based on those for the Easingwold Railway, which had opened in 1891, and the 5½ mile single-track branch was built at a cost of £25,000. Its opening ceremony was on 16th February 1898, when the company's sole engine *Cawood* and two coaches, plus five or six NER coaches, travelled to Cawood and back to Wistow for lunch at the schoolroom!

Goods trains had used the line for some months already, and the first passenger services, five trains each way on weekdays, terminated at a temporary platform at Brayton Gates, ½ mile

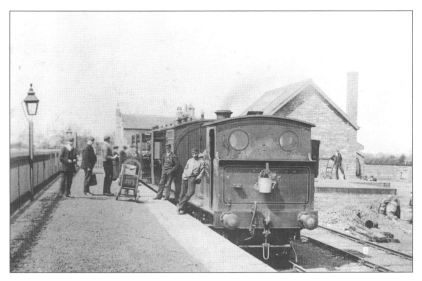

Cawood station around 1907, with NER class H2 0-6-0T no 407, which stayed in service for forty more years. (Stations UK)

121

west of Selby station. This continued even after the NER bought the line for £32,000 in 1900, and it was not until July 1904 that trains ran into Selby. The NER reduced the service to four per day, with an extra on Selby's market day, Monday. In 1908 two petrol-electric autocars were introduced and worked the line's passenger services until 1923. Their replacement was usually an ex-NER 0-6-0T with a single coach, but there was also an experiment with a Leyland rail bus. This had literally been built as a bus for use in Durham, and was converted for the railways at a cost of £425. Based at Selby, this unusual vehicle ran services to Cawood as well as to Goole, York, Castleford and Market Weighton. It was destroyed in a fire at Selby in 1926, and for the final years a steam autocar and Sentinels worked the Cawood line's passenger services, which ended on 31st December 1929.

Freight, chiefly the agricultural produce for which the line was built, continued for the next thirty years, with the occasional outgoing passenger excursion up to about 1946. The track was relaid in 1953, raising hopes that passenger trains might resume,

One of the branch's two NER petro-electric railcars, no 3170, was rescued from a farm near Kirkbymoorside and is shown at Bolton Abbey in April 2004 awaiting restoration. (Author)

The crossing keeper's house at Broad Lane, Cawood is the least-altered of the three that remain. (Author)

but only an 'enthusiasts' special' in April 1960 ventured onto the branch. This was just before final closure on 2nd May, although the very last train was not until 23rd May, when a diesel loco and brake van collected another van and the office furniture from Cawood station. One special passenger on this last trip was John Woodall of Wistow, who had travelled on the first train in 1898. The track was lifted in 1961, and most of the line reverted to farmland. All signs of the railway have disappeared at Cawood, but at Wistow the station building, goods shed and weigh office all still stand, and three of the line's four crossing keepers' houses survive.

Selby to Goole

A third 'lost' line at Selby was a 12-mile branch to the river port of Goole, planned and built in the early years of the 20th century. In 1902 the proposed Selby & Goole Light Railway was to run from the Leeds–Selby line at Selby West, where a connection with the Cawood branch would have been possible, south-east to a separate terminus in Goole. The NER was determined to keep out such competition, and instead proposed a conventional railway along roughly the same route but using the existing station in Goole. This alternative scheme was accepted, although initially the NER built its line to avoid Selby, where the crossing of the Ouse was a major bottleneck. By leaving the Leeds–Selby line at Thorpe Gates Junction, the new route provided a link to Goole for freight traffic, especially coal trains, and opened in December 1910. A spur was also built at Brayton to the Doncaster–Selby line, which allowed passenger services between Selby and Goole to begin on 1st May 1912, calling at intermediate stations at Barlow, Drax Hales and Airmyn & Rawcliffe.

Typical services were three passenger trains each way on weekdays, initially handled by a NER autocar. Journeys were essentially local, with market days at Selby and Goole adding to the traffic, but goods traffic did not meet expectations, and the line was singled soon after the Grouping of 1923. The coal trains

Airmyn & Rawcliffe station in 1958, three years before its name was shortened to Airmyn. (Stations UK)

The line for coal deliveries to Drax power station uses a short stretch of the former trackbed, seen just to the left of one of the cooling towers. (Author)

from the Leeds–Selby line had ended by 1931, when Sentinel railcars handled much of the passenger traffic. Diesel multiple units took over for the last few years, with an increase in services to 5–8 trains daily, but these were withdrawn on 15th June 1964. There is now no trace of the simple wooden station buildings and platforms, but some evidence of the branch remains. The spur from the Doncaster–Selby line remains in use as a siding, and Drax power station's railway uses a short stretch of trackbed, while its access road is built alongside the line's embankment as far as the former Airmyn & Rawcliffe station site.

The Derwent Valley Light Railway

Cliff Common station, 3½ miles along the line from Selby towards Market Weighton, was the starting point for one of the area's few independent railways. Partially opened in 1912, this 16-mile line kept going through the Grouping and nationalisation before its final remnants closed in 1981. Two years after the Light Railways Act of 1896 removed the need for Parliamentary approval, Riccall Rural District Council decided on such a railway, and together with Escrick RDC they obtained authorisation for a line from Cliff Common to Foss Islands in York (rather than Stamford Bridge as originally proposed). This was the only case in Britain of a light railway initiated by its local authorities. Even without Parliament, the procedures took time and it was 1912 before construction started. By then the two councils had transferred their powers to an independent company – the Derwent Valley Light Railway Company (DVLR).

The first 7 miles, from Cliff Common to Wheldrake, opened for goods traffic in October 1912, without any ceremony. This was kept for the formal opening of the whole line on 19th July 1913, when NER 2-2-4T no 1679 with two coaches, two decorated open wagons and a guard's van, steamed away from the company's York station at Layerthorpe. Public services began two days later with three weekday trains each way over

The Foss Islands branch served as the line's link to the rail network at York.
This view is from Layerthorpe bridge, looking north. (J.H. Meredith)

the whole line, plus one between Layerthorpe and Wheldrake only. Intermediate stations were plentiful – Osbaldwick, Murton Lane, Dunnington Halt, Dunnington (for Kexby), Elvington (for Sutton), Wheldrake, Cottingwith, Thorganby, and Skipwith & North Duffield. Times, however, were not reliable, as most trains were 'mixed' and goods wagons had to be added or detached at various stations. In 1915 almost 50,000 passengers were carried; at this time trains ran through to Selby. Ten years later, as bus services took over, this was down to 18,430. For a time in the 1920s the company owned and ran its own engines. For freight there was a petrol shunter and a Sentinel steam loco, while passenger services were handled by a Ford rail bus, with two units that could be used together or singly. After closure to passengers in 1926, this vehicle was sold to the County Donegal Railways in Ireland, and from 1927 all motive power was again hired.

Even after 1926 the line was used by regular excursions, both outgoing to York, Leeds, Harrogate, Bridlington and Scarborough, and incoming, especially at blackberry-picking

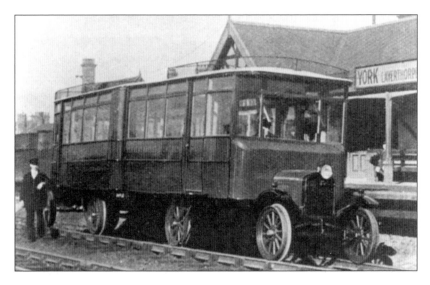

The DVLR's pair of Ford rail bus units, seen at Layerthorpe station in 1924. (Lens of Sutton, courtesy L. Oppitz)

time, with at least eight 'specials' in September 1928. By the 1950s the line's curiosity value attracted railway enthusiasts; 'railtours' ran in 1954, 1958 and 1963, with two in 1965 just before the closure of much of the line. Although it had remained busy for freight, mostly agricultural but also including coal and cement, the post-Beeching closure of the Selby–Market Weighton line ended its southern connection to the national network. The section from Cliff Common to Wheldrake closed in 1965; three years later the line was cut back to Elvington and in 1973 to Dunnington.

The section that remained appeared to have a future, as facilities for oil-storage, coal and cement distribution and grain-drying clustered along its 4¼ miles. Two diesel locos were purchased, 'Light' was dropped from the line's title, and with the opening of the National Railway Museum in York in 1975 its tourist potential was realised. A regular steam service began in 1977 using preserved BR 0-6-0T *Joem*, but only lasted three summers. The industrial use dwindled away, and the last of the line closed in 1981, although the station building and sidings at

Wheldrake station with a railtour headed by class J21 0-6-0 no 65078 in 1954. (Lens of Sutton, courtesy L. Oppitz)

The distinctive design of DVLR stations is clear in this reconstruction of Wheldrake station as 'Murton Park'. (Author)

Layerthorpe were used by British Rail for another eight years. The station building at Wheldrake was rebuilt as 'Murton Park' at the Yorkshire Museum of Farming, where a ¾ mile section of the DVLR line had been retained for trips, some steam-hauled, on summer Sundays. Further west, the trackbed from Osbaldwick to Layerthorpe, along with the former Foss Islands branch, was converted into a footpath and cycleway by Sustrans in 1992.

12
Holderness

The Withernsea branch
The Hornsea branch

A fine survivor of both lines – the Wilmington swing bridge of 1907, still movable for river traffic but now used only by pedestrians and cyclists. (Author)

The Withernsea branch

Holderness is the low-lying area between the Yorkshire Wolds and the North Sea. On its rapidly retreating coastline lie the small seaside resorts of Hornsea and Withernsea, formerly linked to Hull by separate branch lines. Withernsea's was the first to be built, under the name Hull & Holderness Railway, and opened in 1854 as one of the area's few truly independent lines,

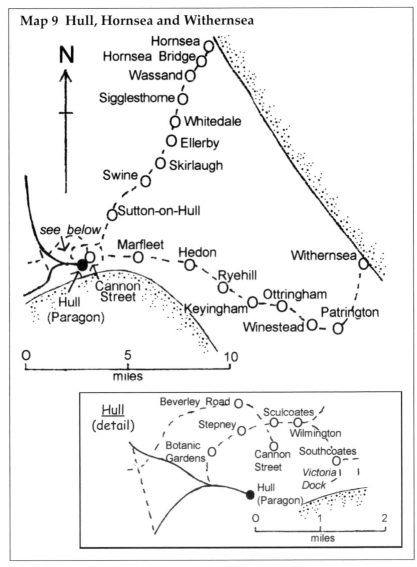

Map 9 Hull, Hornsea and Withernsea

with its own engines, carriages and wagons. It was promoted by a Hull businessman, Anthony Bannister, who dreamed of the small village of Withernsea (with a population of 109 in 1851) becoming a northern Brighton. Construction was easy as the

The well-preserved Stepney station building still survives from the Y&NM's 1853 Victoria Dock branch. (Author)

route was mostly on low land close to the River Humber, and the line was completed in eleven months, but access into Hull was not so straightforward. The city's first rail link was west from a terminus on Manor House Street, built by the Hull & Selby Railway Company in 1840 but leased to the York & North Midland (Y&NM) five years later. In 1853 the Y&NM opened a line from Manor House Street round Hull's northern suburbs to Victoria Dock, with intermediate stations at Stepney, Sculcoates and Southcoates. There were also various stopping points; one of these, Cemetery Gates, became an additional station in 1866 which was eventually renamed Botanic Gardens. The Hull & Holderness used this branch's eastern section to Victoria Dock for its first access into the city.

After the Withernsea line's opening ceremony on 26th June 1854, public services began the next day with five or six trains each way daily, stopping at intermediate stations at Marfleet, Hedon, Ryehill, Keyingham, Ottringham, Winestead (closed to passengers in 1904) and Patrington. Over 63,000 people travelled

A loco is being turned on Withernsea's turntable in this scene from 1906, with the station at the far right and the Convalescent Home, built as the Station Hotel, on the left. (Memory Lane, Hull)

on the line in its first four months, but its development was handicapped by its single track and inconvenient terminus. These may have contributed to the loss of the line's independence; it was leased by the NER in 1860 and absorbed two years later. The NER solved the access problem in 1864 by doubling the Victoria Dock branch (except for the bridge over the River Hull at Wilmington), and constructing a new connecting curve, which allowed trains from Withernsea to use the Victoria Dock branch westwards into Hull Paragon station. Its 'suburban' service, which had been withdrawn in 1854, was revived and incorporated into the services to Withernsea and Hornsea.

The bridge at Wilmington remained a bottleneck, as trains had to be guided across its single track by a pilotman. In 1907 the NER replaced it with a new double-track bridge, and around that time also doubled much of the track out to Withernsea. However, the Hedon–Ryehill and Ottringham–Winestead sections remained single-track, hindering the line's further development. Its heyday was probably the 1930s, following the

Station staff had assembled for this early 20th century view of Patrington station. (Author's collection)

'Highflyer', seen here at Hull, was one of the Sentinel steam railcars used on both the Withernsea and Hornsea lines in the 1930s. (Author's collection)

introduction in 1929 of the 'Hull and District Interval Service'. The LNER's new timetable was based on departures at regular intervals to Beverley, Brough, South Howden, Withernsea and Hornsea. The latter two destinations had an hourly service at 40 and 50 minutes past the hour respectively, with about half the journeys made by Sentinel steam railcars. The first twelve months for the whole area showed increases in passenger journeys of 16% and revenue of 6%, but the increased competition from buses and the depression of the 1930s eventually put paid to the scheme.

Attempts to boost the Withernsea line continued after World War II. There were plans to revive Hedon Racecourse, which had had a short-lived station in the 1900s, and a speedway track built in the late 1940s had its own halt. In 1957 the line had some of the area's first diesel multiple unit services, which from 1960 were operated as 'Paytrains' with conductor/guards issuing tickets. This allowed the intermediate stations to be unstaffed, but still the line lost money and was listed for closure in the Beeching Report. The end for passenger services came on 17th October 1964, and for goods east of Hedon seven months later. In 1968 Hedon goods depot shut, and all remaining freight was switched to the former Hull & Barnsley high-level route round northern Hull. This allowed the closure of the Victoria Dock branch with its six level crossings, much to the relief of Hull's motorists, although the last section of the Withernsea line, Southcoates–Marfleet, remained in use for freight until 1972. Since closure much of the former Victoria Dock branch route has become a footpath, and the Withernsea branch from East Hull to Winestead is now officially a cycle path. However, this is not as well used or maintained as its ex-Hornsea line equivalent and is difficult to follow, especially at its eastern end.

The Hornsea branch

The 13-mile line to Hornsea had many similarities to the Withernsea branch, but was opened later (1864) and was more difficult to build. Away from the Humber, Holderness is covered by glacial clays, which provided such an unstable foundation that embankments and a viaduct needed to be rebuilt. Perhaps influenced by the earlier Withernsea line, the Hull & Hornsea Railway Company was only nominally independent, and from the start its operations were worked by the NER, with full takeover in 1866. Again there were initial problems with the access into Hull, trains terminating originally at Wilmington, just before the junction with the Victoria Dock branch. This was the starting point for the sixteen-coach train used for the opening ceremony on Easter Monday, 28th March 1864, but within four months trains from Hornsea were able to run into Paragon station at Hull.

The line did not tap into the expanding dock areas east of Hull and instead headed north-east across farming areas to Hornsea, which was already established as a small town and appears not to have welcomed the railway as much as Withernsea. The line has been described as 'littered with stations', and their history is complicated by closures and name changes. Starting at the Hull end, the original Wilmington was closed in 1912 and replaced, together with Sculcoates on the Victoria Dock branch, by a new

The crossing gates and their operator feature clearly in this early view of Swine station. (Author's collection)

The overall roof of Hornsea Town station is well shown in this 1962 scene, two years before closure. (D. Thompson)

Wilmington station was a 1912 replacement but all that is left is the former ticket office, now used as a workmen's cafe. (Author)

Wilmington station. The next stations were Sutton-on-Hull, Swine and Skirlaugh, which remained unaltered during the line's existence. Ellerby, however, closed in 1902, and its name was reused twenty years later for the next station, which had previously been called Marton, then Burton Constable! Whitedale and Sigglesthorne stations came next, followed by Goxhill, renamed Wassand in 1904. This was one of the last 'Market Day Only' stations in north-east England, with just a single train each way calling on Mondays only. Hornsea was provided with two stations; Hornsea Bridge was meant to be the original terminus but a ½ mile extension, built with some difficulty, took the line to a fine terminus at Hornsea (Hornsea Town from 1950).

In the 1900s the track appears to have been doubled, allowing services by 1914 to increase to fourteen each way on weekdays and, unusually for the NER, two on Sundays. Like the Withernsea branch, the line gained hourly trains with the introduction of the 'Hull and District Interval Service' in 1929, but by 1942 the service was down to nine or ten a day. The postwar improvements of diesel multiple units and 'Paytrains' failed to halt the decline in usage, with Wassand station shutting to passengers in 1953 and Skirlaugh four years later. Full closure of the branch to passengers came on 17th October 1964, and to freight over almost all the line in 1965. The route has remained more intact than that to Withernsea; most of its stations survive, with the former Hornsea Town building a particularly fine example of restoration. Hornsea Bridge station did not survive (along with Skirlaugh and Sutton-on-Hull), but its site marks the end of 12 miles of continuous cycle route on the former trackbed, which is now part of the TransPennine Trail.

13
The Hull & Barnsley Railway
Hull Cannon Street to Carlton Towers

The dingy surroundings of Hull's Cannon Street station around 1939. By then it had only been used for goods for about fifteen years. (Stations UK)

Apart from the Midland in the far west and south-west, the only company to seriously challenge the late 19th century NER monopoly in this area was the Hull & Barnsley Railway (H&B). Described as 'one of the last complete and independent Victorian railways', it survived for thirty-seven years of operations before being swallowed up by the NER in 1922. Ironically it was at Hull's NER-owned Station Hotel in 1879 that a group of businessmen set up the 'Hull, Barnsley & West Riding Junction Railway and Dock Company' (the name was not officially shortened until 1905). The 53 mile main line received its Act in 1880, and opened five years later at a cost of over £4

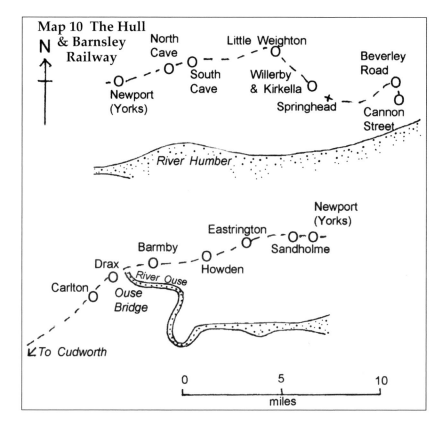

Map 10 The Hull & Barnsley Railway

million, making it one of the most expensive railways ever built in this country. The main problem was that the NER's Hull–Selby line had taken the low ground by the Humber estuary, leaving the H&B to find a route through the hills of the Yorkshire Wolds further north. This required many embankments and cuttings (the longest at Little Weighton over ¾ mile long) and three tunnels, two of them short but the third, Drewton, 2,116 yards in length. Even so the line still rose to a summit at 250 ft, requiring double-heading for many of the coal trains that were the mainstay of its freight traffic.

Lack of finance was always a problem for the new company and caused plans for a city centre station in Hull to be abandoned. Instead its terminus was based on its carriage sheds

A 1972 view of the steam-powered swing bridge over the River Ouse, demolished four years later. (J.H. Meredith)

at Cannon Street, described as 'a seedy part of town' and hardly encouraging for passengers. This was reached by a spur from the company's freight line, which went around northern Hull to its Alexandra Dock, then the largest in Hull and opened just before the railway itself. There was a special passenger train from Hull to Stairfoot near Barnsley on 25th May 1885, but it was 27th July before regular services began with thirteen weekday trains and four on Sundays. Substantial stations were provided at Beverley Road in north Hull, Willerby & Kirkella, Little Weighton, South Cave, North Cave, Newport, Sandholme, Eastrington, Howden, Barmby, Drax and Carlton, before the railway entered South Yorkshire en route for Cudworth. This was as close to Barnsley as the line got, but it did provide access to the Midland system. In 1905 running powers to Sheffield were obtained, and a service of three trains a day lasted until 1917.

It is difficult to weigh up the success or otherwise of the H&B's battle with the NER over freight, although matters improved after a working agreement in 1899. However, there can be little doubt as to its failure as a passenger operation; for the first twenty years only four-wheeled carriages were used, and there are claims of three-coach trains arriving at Cannon Street without a single passenger. By 1922 only two of the nine weekday trains went beyond Howden to Cudworth, and in April of that year the H&B was finally absorbed by the NER, itself soon to be part of the LNER. This led to several name changes; Newport became Wallingfen, Eastrington and Howden added 'North' and 'South' respectively, Drax 'Abbey' and Carlton 'Towers'. More importantly in 1924 the LNER opened a link into Hull Paragon station, and closed Beverley Road and Cannon Street to passengers. In 1928 Sentinel steam railcars were introduced, and the following year the eastern part of the line became part of the 'Hull and District Interval Service'. This provided hourly trains to South Howden, with an additional unstaffed halt at Springhead, close to the former H&B workshops. The line west to Cudworth was not included, and in

Class G5 no 67282 with a Hull–North Cave train in 1955 at Springhead halt. When opened in 1929 this was regarded as possibly Britain's smallest station. (Memory Lane, Hull)

South Howden became the western passenger terminus in 1931 and is seen here with class G5 no 67253 (formerly on the Pateley Bridge branch) in April 1955, only three months before closure. (Author's collection)

1932 it became the first British main line to lose its passenger services. Those to South Howden lingered on, down to four to seven trains on weekdays only by 1955. The last scheduled passenger train, the 8.30 pm from Hull to South Howden ran on July 30th that year. Surprisingly the line was still open to Cudworth for freight, which lasted over the whole line until 1958. The pick-up goods service then ended in stages, the last section, Springhead to Little Weighton, closing in 1964.

The former line has some splendid surviving station buildings, notably South Cave, one of the line's two highest category stations, and Drax, where the goods shed and crossing keeper's house also still stand. Past nearby Carlton, where the building is another survivor, run almost 4 miles of track, part of the route serving Europe's largest power station at Drax. Other station sites have been lost completely, including

144

The H&B has left several fine station buildings, including the one at Little Weighton shown here. (Author)

The abandoned trackbed west of Sugar Loaf Tunnel, showing the difficult terrain tackled by the H&B. (Author)

Newport/Wallingfen now under the M62 motorway. The trackbed can be walked at Eastrington and Springhead, but best of all is the section through the Wolds to the entrance of Sugar Loaf Tunnel. The most surprising survival is the freight line through northern Hull (which also provided access to Cannon Street station). After many years of delay, in 1968 this became the preferred route to Hull's eastern docks, allowing the ex-NER Victoria Dock branch to close. Perhaps the backers of the H&B had been justified after all!

Conclusion

At the time of the Grouping in 1923, the railway network in North and East Yorkshire was at its greatest extent. There were around 900 miles in passenger use, with well over 300 stations. Today, there are about 385 miles still in use, with 80 stations, as part of the national network, not including preservation schemes. This somewhat hides the paucity of routes remaining; away from the East Coast Main Line, over most of the area there are only lines to the major centres of Hull, Harrogate, Scarborough and Middlesbrough, apart from the surprising survival of one route to Whitby. So what happened to the rest?

Many people's answer would probably be the single word 'Beeching', referring to the man behind the infamous report titled 'The Reshaping of British Railways', published in 1963. However, a study of the figures reveals some interesting facts. In the forty years up to 1963, almost 300 miles of line closed to passengers, along with 173 stations (over half the 1923 total). By comparison, closures resulting from the Beeching proposals totalled 205 miles and a mere 60 stations. As in other areas, the Beeching closures continued a pattern of withdrawal of services that had begun much earlier.

To understand the impact of the Beeching Report, we need to take a closer look at the lines involved in the closures. Apart from the former Hull & Barnsley Railway, which was regarded in some railway circles as merely duplicating existing routes, closures before 1963 were mostly rural branches. They included the three independent lines, and several other lines to minor country termini such as Masham, Cawood and Pateley Bridge. Even where they provided possible through routes, as in Wensleydale for example, their potential had not been developed. Apart from the former iron-mining settlements between Guisborough and Loftus, the largest places left without a rail link as a result of the pre-1963 closures were Easingwold, Bedale and Stokesley, each with a population today of only three to four thousand. Moreover the withdrawals were staggered, beginning in the 1920s with the Derwent Valley and Nidd Valley light railways, and continuing up to the Guisborough–Loftus line in 1960.

The picture is very different for the Beeching closures. First the places involved were larger; Ripon, Guisborough and Whitby (where full closure was proposed but not implemented) were all substantial settlements with well over 10,000 inhabitants, and another eight towns at 4–10,000 lost their rail services as well. Secondly the lines involved were not mostly rural branches, but often once-important secondary routes. The most outstanding example would be the Harrogate–Ripon–Northallerton line, which up to 1964 had a daily Pullman express and even until closure through services from Liverpool and Manchester to Newcastle. In addition such lines were seen to be part of a national network, not just branch lines to country termini. The effect of the Beeching cuts was to remove the railways from large areas of Yorkshire; Map 7 well illustrates this with the Market Weighton district, where an area well over 400 square miles has been left with only disused lines. Lastly the time scale was also very different; despite objections and hearings, all the area's Beeching line closures to passengers occurred within two years, except Harrogate–Ripon–Northallerton and the Richmond branch (both shut by the end of the decade).

So what have the 515 or so miles of disused railway left behind? It has to be said that there is comparatively little in terms of walkable trackbed, viaducts and tunnels. There are exceptions; the viaducts at Stamford Bridge and Larpool near Whitby can be walked, and the Scarborough–Whitby, Hull–Hornsea and Market Weighton–Beverley trackbeds are all well preserved. Elsewhere the abandoned lines have largely returned to farmland and in many cases are difficult to trace. In terms of stations, however, the area has fared better; at a conservative estimate over 90 station buildings survive in good condition. This does not include the ten restored by the end of 2004 as part of the area's railway preservation schemes. It is here that the 'lost railways' can best be experienced. With the expansions currently planned, these schemes will also help return parts of the lost railway network of North and East Yorkshire to the national scene.

Opening and Final Closure Dates of Lines to Regular Passenger Traffic

Line	Opened	Final Closure
Grosmont/Pickering	26.5.1836	8.3.1965
Pickering/Malton	7.7.1845	8.3.1965
Richmond branch	10.9.1846	3.3.1969
Boroughbridge/Pilmoor	17.6.1847	25.9.1950
York/Market Weighton	3.10.1847	29.11.1965
Selby/Market Weighton	1.8.1848	14.6.1965
Church Fenton/Harrogate	20.7.1848[1]	6.1.1964
Thirsk/Melmerby/Starbeck	14.9.1848[1]	6.3.1967[2]
Melmerby/Northallerton	2.6.1852	6.3.1967
Pilmoor/Gilling/Malton	20.5.1853	2.2.1953[3]
Malton/Driffield	1.6.1853	5.6.1950
Victoria Dock branch (Hull)	1.6.1853	19.10.1964
Nunthorpe Junction/Guisborough	25.2.1854	2.3.1964
Hull/Withernsea	27.6.1854	19.10.1964
Picton/Battersby	1.4.1861[1]	14.6.1954
Pateley Bridge branch	1.5.1862	2.4.1951
Hull/Hornsea	29.3.1864	19.10.1964
Market Weighton/Beverley	1.5.1865	29.11.1965
Selby/York	2.1.1871	3.10.1983
Knaresborough/Boroughbridge	1.4.1875	25.9.1950
Gilling/Pickering	1.4.1875[1]	2.2.1953
Saltburn/Loftus	1.4.1875	10.9.1951[4]
Melmerby/Masham	9.6.1875	1.1.1931
Northallerton/Hawes	1.10.1878[1]	26.4.1954
Hawes/Garsdale	1.10.1878	16.3.1959
Guisborough/Brotton	1.11.1878	2.5.1960
Pickering/Seamer	1.5.1882	5.6.1950

Whitby/Loftus	3.12.1883	5.5.1958[5]
Scarborough/Whitby	16.7.1885	8.3.1965
Hull/Cudworth	27.7.1885	1.1.1932[6]
Skipton/Ilkley	1.10.1888[1]	22.3.1965
Market Weighton/Driffield	1.5.1890	14.6.1965
Alne/Easingwold	27.7.1891	29.11.1948
Selby/Cawood	16.2.1898	1.1.1930
Skipton/Grassington	29.7.1902	22.9.1930
Nidd Valley Light Railway	12.9.1907	1.1.1930
Selby/Goole	1.5.1912	15.6.1964
Derwent Valley Light Railway	21.7.1913	1.9.1926
Catterick Camp Military Railway	October 1916	26.10.1964
Filey Holiday Camp branch	summer 1946	17.9.1977

Note: Closure dates are those posted by the operating company, usually a Monday, with the last train on the previous Saturday or Sunday. Reopenings by preservation societies have not been included.

1 Opened in stages to this date
2 Thirsk/Melmerby had already closed 14.9.1959
3 Gilling/Malton had already closed 30.12.1930
4 Brotton/Loftus remained open until 2.5.1960
5 Whitby West Cliff station remained open until 12.6.1961 and the line from there to Whitby Town until 8.3.1965
6 Services from Hull to South Howden continued until 1.8.1955

Bibliography

Many of the following are out of print but can still be obtained second-hand or consulted in libraries.

Bairstow, Martin *Railways Around Harrogate, Volumes 1–3* (Martin Bairstow)

Bairstow, Martin *Railways Around Whitby, Volumes 1–2* (Martin Bairstow)

Binns, Donald *The Yorkshire Dales Railway: The Grassington Branch* (Northern Heritage)

Burton, Warwick *The Malton and Driffield Railway* (Martin Bairstow)

Chapman, Stephen *Hudson's Way (The story of the York–Beverley railway)* (York Railpress)

Croft, D.J. *The Nidd Valley Light Railway* (Oakwood Press)

Goode, C.T. *The Goole and Selby Railway* (Oakwood Press)

Goode, C.T. *The Railways of East Yorkshire* (Oakwood Press)

Goode, C.T. *The Selby and Driffield Railway* (C.T. Goode)

Hartley, K.E *The Cawood, Wistow and Selby Light Railway* (Turntable Enterprises)

Hartley, K.E. *The Easingwold Railway* (Oakwood Press)

Hoole, K. *A Regional History of the Railways of Great Britain: Volume 4: North East England* (David & Charles)

Hoole, K. *Forgotten Railways: North East England* (David & Charles)

Hoole, K. *Railways in Cleveland* (Dalesman Books)

Hoole, K. *Railways in the Yorkshire Dales* (Dalesman Books)

Hoole, K. *The Whitby, Redcar and Middlesbrough Union Railway* (Hendon Publishing)

Howat, Patrick *The Pilmoor, Boroughbridge and Knaresborough Railway* (Martin Bairstow)

Howat, Patrick *The Railways of Ryedale* (Martin Bairstow)

Jenkins, Stanley *The Wensleydale Railway: A New History* (Oakwood Press)

Joy, David *Whitby and Pickering Railway* (Dalesman Books)

Lidster, J. Robin *The Forge Valley Line* (Hendon Publishing)
Lidster, J. Robin *The Scarborough & Whitby Railway* (Hendon Publishing)
Ludlam, A.J. *The Catterick Camp Military Railway and the Richmond Branch* (Oakwood Press)
Reading, S.J. *The Derwent Valley Railway* (Oakwood Press)
Redman, Ronald Nelson *Railway Byways in Yorkshire* (Dalesman Books)
Rogers, James *Railways of Harrogate & District* (North Eastern Railway Association)
Smith, F.W. and Binns, D. *Railways in the Northern Dales 1: The Skipton and Ilkley Line* (Wyvern Publications)

Details of the following lines not covered in this book can be found as follows:

The Rosedale mineral railway – *Railways in Cleveland* (above); also Hayes, R.H. and Rutter, J.G. *Rosedale Mines and Railway* (Scarborough Archaeological and Historical Society)
The Sand Hutton line – Hartley, K.E. *The Sand Hutton Light Railway* (The Narrow Gauge Railway Society*)*
The Spurn Head line – Hartley, K.E. and Frost, H.M. *The Spurn Head Railway* (The Industrial Railway Society)

Details of the preservation schemes can be found at the following websites:

www.embsayboltonabbeyrailway.org.uk
www.northyorkshiremoorsrailway.com
www.wensleydalerailway.com

Index

Addingham 12, 14
Ainderby 54, 55
Airmyn & Rawcliffe 124 *seq*
Alne 42, 43
Amotherby 97
Ampleforth 97, 98; College 93, 98
Andrews, George 10, 25, 49, 54, 82
Askrigg 55
Aysgarth 55, 58

Bainton 112 *seq*
Baldersby 27, 28
Bannister, Anthony 132
Barlby 119, 120
Barlow 124
Barmby 142
Barnsley 142
Barton-le-Street 97
Battersby (formerly Ingleby Junction, then Battersby Junction) 60–64, 89
Beckhole 86 *seq*
Bedale 54, 55, 59, 147
Bedale & Leyburn Railway 54
Beeching Report 14, 26, 30, 89, 110, 128, 136, 147, 148
Bell, William 10
Beverley 108–113, 136, 148
Beverley Road, Hull 142, 143
Bilton Junction 28
Birkinshaw, John 104

Birstwith 36, 37
Bishophouse Junction 97
Bolton Abbey 11–17, 122
'Bonnyface', the 55, 56
Boosbeck 68, 72
Boroughbridge 30–33
Botanic Gardens, Hull 133
Boulby 72, 82
Bradford 12 *seq*, 37 *seq*; Corporation 37; Waterworks Committee 40
Brafferton 30, 31, 33
Bramhope Tunnel 23
Brampton Road 51, 52
Brayton 124
Brayton Gates 121
Bridlington 84, 114, 127
Brotton 68 *seq*
Brough 136
Bubwith 113; Trail 116
Burdale 107; Tunnel 105
Burnby (see Nunburnholme)
Burton Constable 139
Butlins, Filey 10, 82–84, 107, 114

California 51
Camp Centre, Catterick 50, 51
Carlin How Viaduct 72
Carlton (later Carlton Towers) 142, 143, 144
Castleford 122
Catterick Bridge 46, 49 *seq*

Catterick Camp 10, 49, 58;
    Military Railway 50–52
Cawood 121–124, 147
Cawood & Wistow Light
    Railway 121
Cemetery Gates, Hull (later
    Botanic Gardens) 133
Chaloner Whin Junction 119
Cherry Burton 108, 110
Church Fenton 21–27
Cleveland Railway 66–68, 75
Cliff Common (Gate) 113, 126,
    128
Cloughton 78
Cod Hill 65
Colne 11, 13
Constable Burton 55
Copgrove (formerly 'and
    Staveley') 31, 33
Cottingworth 127
Coxwold 97
Crakehall 55
Crimple Viaduct 27
Croft Spa 46
Cross Gates 23, 26
Cudworth 142 *seq*

Dacre 35–37
Darley 36, 37
Darlington 31, 46 *seq*, 52, 99
Derwent Valley Light Railway
    (DVLR) 10, 126–130, 148
Dickens, Alfred 104
Doncaster 119, 120, 124, 126
Dragon Junction 28
Drax (later Drax Abbey) 142 *seq*
Drax Hales 124
Drax power station 125, 126,
    144

Drewton Tunnel 141
Driffield 97, 103–107, 108,
    113–116
Duffield Gate 113
Dunnington 127, 128; Halt 127

Earswick (Huntington) 108
Easington (later Grinkle) 75
Easingwold 41–44, 147;
    Railway 41–44, 121
East Coast Main Line 26, 27,
    30, 31, 42, 46, 52, 54, 59, 96,
    99, 117 *seq*, 147
Eastrington (later North
    Eastrington) 142, 143, 146
Ebberston (formerly Wilton)
    94, 96
Ellerby 139
Elvington 127, 128
Embsay 12, 14–16, 17
Embsay & Bolton Abbey
    Steam Railway 11, 14–17
Enthorpe 103, 113 *seq*
Eryholme Junction (formerly
    Dalton Junction) 46
Escrick 119, 120
Esk Valley 88
Eston 67
Everingham (formerly
    Harswell Gate) 113

Falsgrave Tunnel 78
Fangoss 108, 110
Filey Holiday Camp branch
    10, 82–84, 99
Finghall Lane 55
Foggathorpe (Gate) 113
Forge Valley 94; Line 10,
    93–96; Railway 94

Foss Islands 126 *seq*
Fyling Hall 78

Garsdale 53–57, 59
Garton 105
Gate Helmsley (see Holtby)
Gilling 96–102
Gilling & Pickering line 97,
  100–102
Goathland (formerly
  Goathland Mill) 86 *seq*
Goole 121 124–126
Goxhill (see Wassand)
Grassington branch 14, 17–20
Grassington & Threshfield 18
Great Northern Railway
  (GNR) 23, 28, 119
Great North of England
  Railway 27, 30, 46
Grinkle (formerly Easington)
  75, 76; Tunnel 75
Grosmont 62, 85–92; Tunnel
  86, 87
Guisborough 65–72, 73, 76,
  147, 148

Hampsthwaite 36, 37
Harrogate 9, 12, 13, 21–33, 36
  seq, 127, 147, 148;
  Brunswick 22, 23
Hawes 44, 53–57, 59; Junction
  55
Hawes & Melmerby Railway
  44, 54
Hawsker 78, 82
Hayburn Wyke 78
Hedon 133 *seq*; Racecourse 136
Hellifield 17, 55
Helmsley 94, 100 *seq*

High Field (formerly Bubwith
  High Field) 113
Hinderwell 75
Holme Moor (formerly
  Holme) 113, 115
Holtby (Gate Helmsley) 108,
  110
Holywell 14
Hornsea 131, 135, 136–139,
  148; Town 138, 139; Bridge
  139
Hovingham Spa (formerly
  Hovingham) 97
Howden (later South
  Howden) 113, 142, 143
Hudson, George 9, 10, 22, 27,
  54, 103, 108, 118
Hudson Way 110
Hull 9, 10, 78, 103, 108 *seq*, 114,
  120, 131 *seq*, 140–146, 147,
  148; Cannon Street 140 *seq*;
  Paragon 10, 134, 137, 143
Hull & Barnsley Railway
  (H&B) 108, 136, 140–146,
  147
Hull and District Interval
  Service 136, 139, 143
Hull & Holderness Railway
  131, 133
Hull & Hornsea Railway 137
Hull & Selby Railway 119, 133
Hull, Barnsley & West Riding
  Junction Railway and Dock
  Company 140
Huntington (see Earswick)
Husthwaite Gate 97
Hutton Gate 65, 67

Ilkley 11–14

Ingleby 62, 64; Junction 62
Ingleton 11

Jervaulx (formerly Newton-le-Willows) 55

Kettleness 75 *seq*; Tunnel 74
Keyingham 133
Killinghall (see Ripley Valley)
Kilton Viaduct 68
Kiplingcotes 108, 110, 111
Kirbymoorside 100, 101
Kirkbymoorside (see also Kirbymoorside) 100, 102, 122
Knaresborough 30–33, 34
Knottingley 119

Lancashire & Yorkshire Railway 13
Larpool Viaduct 78, 81, 82, 148
Layerthorpe 126 *seq*
Leeds 12 *seq*, 23, 27, 37, 100, 114, 124, 126, 127
Leeds & Bradford Railway 11
Leeds & Thirsk Railway (L&T) 9, 23, 27, 28, 36
Leeds Northern (LN) 9, 27, 62
Leeming 54, 59; Bar (formerly Leeming Lane) 55, 58
Levisham 86, 91
Leyburn 44, 53 *seq*
Lingthorpe Junction 60
Little Weighton 141, 142, 144
Lofthouse-in-Nidderdale (formerly Lofthouse) 37, 38, 40
Loftus (formerly Lofthouse) 66, 68–72, 73–77, 79, 147, 148

Londesborough (Shipton) 108, 112
London & North Eastern Railway (LNER) 9, 10, 13, 46, 51, 80, 96, 119, 136, 143
London, Midland & Scottish Railway (LMS) 10, 56

Malton 85 *seq*, 94, 96–99, 103–107
Malton & Driffield Junction Railway (M&D) 9, 97, 99, 103 *seq*, 108
'Malton Dodger' 106
Manor House Street, Hull 133
Marfleet 133, 136
Marishes Road 87
Market Weighton 108–116, 122, 128, 148
Marton 139
Masham 44–46, 147
Melmerby (formerly Wath) 27 *seq*, 41, 44–46
Menthorpe Gate 113, 114
Metropolitan Railway 38
Midland & NER Joint line 12
Midland Railway 10, 11 *seq*, 54, 55, 142
Middlesbrough (formerly Port Darlington) 9, 49, 62 *seq*, 65–67, 68, 70, 75 *seq*, 89, 147
Middlesbrough & Guisborough Railway (M&G) 65–67
Middleton-on-the-Wolds 113
Moulton 46
Murton Lane 127

Naburn 119, 120

National Railway Museum, York 128
Nawton 100, 101
Newby Wiske 27, 28
Newcastle 103, 105, 148
Newcastle & Darlington Junction Railway 54, 96
Newcastle-upon-Tyne & Hull Direct Railway 103
Newport (later Wallingfen) 142, 143, 146
Newtondale halt 91
Newton Kyme 23, 24, 25, 27, 112
Nidd Bridge (formerly Ripley) 27, 30
Nidd Valley Light Railway (NVLR) 10, 37–40, 148
Normanton 118
Northallerton 27–30, 53–59, 62, 148
North Cave 142, 143
North Eastern Railway (NER) 9, 10, 13, 23, 27, 36, 37, 42, 44, 46, 54 *seq*, 62, 66, 68, 70, 74, 78, 87, 91, 94, 97, 100, 103, 107, 108, 113, 116, 119 *seq*, 134, 137, 139, 140 *seq*
North Grimston 105
North Skelton 68, 70, 72
North Yorkshire & Cleveland Railway (NY&C) 62
North Yorkshire Moors Railway 85, 89, 90–92
Nunburnholme (Burnby) 108, 110
Nunnington 100, 101
Nunthorpe 62, 65; Junction 67

Ormesby 65, 66
Osbaldwick 127, 130
Otley 13
Ottringham 133 *seq*

Pateley Bridge branch 10, 34–40, 144, 147
Patrington 133, 135
Peak 78
Pickering 85–92, 93–102
Pickhill 27, 28
Picton 60–64
Pilmoor 30–33, 96–99; Curve 97, 100
Pinchinthorpe 65, 67
Pocklington 10, 108
Port Darlington (see Middlesbrough)
Potto 62, 64
Priestcroft Curve 68
Prosser, Thomas 10

Ramsgill 38, 40
Ravenscar (formerly Peak) 78, 112
Redcar 62, 67
Redmire 55 *seq*
Ricall 119, 120
Richmond 10, 46–50, 51, 148
Rillington 87, 89, 94; Junction 92
Ripley (see Nidd Bridge)
Ripley Junction 36
Ripley Valley (formerly Killinghall) 36
Ripon 27–30, 46, 148
Robin Hood's Bay 78, 80
Rosedale mines 10, 62, 64
Ruswarp 86

Ryedale Railway 100
Ryehill 133, 134
Rylstone 17, 18, 20

Saltburn 49, 62, 68–72, 75, 78
Sand Hutton Railway 10
Sandholme 142
Sandsend 74 *seq*; Tunnel 77
Sawdon 94, 95
Scalby 78, 80; Viaduct 78, 82
Scarborough 9, 10, 70, 75 *seq*,
  78–84, 88, 92, 94 *seq*, 113,
  114, 127, 147, 148
Scarborough & Whitby
  Railway Company 78
Scarborough, Bridlington &
  West Riding Junction
  Railway (SB&WRJ) 113
Scarborough Road Junction
  97, 99, 104
Scorton 46
Scruton 53, 55
Sculcoates 133, 137
Seamer Junction 94
Selby 113–116, 117–130, 141
Selby & Goole Light Railway
  124
Selby & Mid-Yorkshire Union
  Railway 121
Settle 11 *seq*
Settle & Carlisle (S&C) 17, 54,
  55, 57, 58
Settrington 105
Sexhow 62, 64
Shaftholme Junction 119
Sheffield 142
Shipton (see Londesborough)
Sigglesthorne 139
Sinderby 27, 28, 30

Sinnington 100
Skinningrove 68, 70, 72
Skipton 11–20
Skipwith & North Duffield
  127
Skirlaugh 139
Skythorn Quarry 20
Sledmere & Fimber (formerly
  Fimber) 105 *seq*, 112
Sleights 86
Slingsby 97, 98
Snainton 94
Southburn 113
South Cave 142, 144
Southcoates 133, 136
South Howden 136, 143, 144
Spennithorne 55
Spofforth 22, 23, 27
Springhead 143, 144, 146
Spurn Head Railway 10
Staintondale 78, 81
Stairfoot 142
Staithes 73 *seq*; Viaduct 74
Stamford Bridge 108, 109, 126;
  Viaduct 110, 148
Starbeck 23, 27, 30, 46
Stephenson, George 9, 86
Stepney 133
Stockton (see Warthill)
Stockton & Darlington
  Railway 9, 34, 62, 65
Stockton-on-Tees 27, 62
Stokesley 60–64, 147
Stutton 23, 27
Sugar Loaf tunnel 145, 146
Sutton-on-Hull 139
Swinden Quarry 19, 20
Swine 137, 139

Tadcaster 23, 26, 27
Tanfield 45, 46
Telford, Thomas 34
Thirsk 27–30, 97, 98, 102
Thirsk & Malton Railway
  (T&M) 30, 96, 99, 100, 102,
  104 *seq*
Thorganby 127
Thornton Dale 94, 96
Thorp Arch 23, 26, 27
Thorpe Gates Junction 124
Topcliffe 27, 28
TransPennine Trail 139
Trenholme Bar 62

Upleatham Viaduct 68, 72

Victoria Dock, Hull 133 *seq*,
  146

Wallingfen 143
Warthill (Stockton) 108, 110
Wassand (formerly Goxhill)
  139
Waterfall Viaduct 71, 72
Wath (later Melmerby) 27
Wath-in-Nidderdale 38, 40
Wensley 55
Wensleydale Railway 10,
  58–59; Association 58
West Hartlepool Harbour &
  Railway Company 66
Wetherby 23 *seq*; Racecourse
  26
Wetwang 105

Wharram 105, 107
Wheldrake 126 *seq*
Whitby 41, 62 *seq*, 73–82, 86
  seq, 94, 147, 148; West Cliff
  75, 77, 78; Town 75, 78, 82
Whitby & Pickering Railway
  (W&P) 9, 62, 86 *seq*
Whitby, Redcar &
  Middlesbrough Union
  Railway (WR&MU) 73 *seq*
Whitedale 139
Whorlton 62
Willerby & Kirkella 142
Wilmington 137 *seq*; bridge
  131, 134
Winestead 133, 134, 136
Wistow 121, 124
Withernsea 131-136
Wormald Green 27, 29, 30
Wykeham 94. 96

York 9, 10, 13, 78, 87, 88, 92, 94
  seq, 108–113, 117–120, 122,
  127
York & North Midland
  Railway (Y&NM) 9, 22 *seq*,
  87, 94, 108, 113, 118, 133
York & Selby Railway Path
  120
York, Newcastle & Berwick
  Railway 9
Yorkshire Dales Railway 14,
  17
Yorkshire Museum of
  Farming 130